A scene from the New York production of *Based on a Totally True Story*.

BASED ON
A TOTALLY
TRUE STORY

BY ROBERTO AGUIRRE-SACASA

★

DRAMATISTS
PLAY SERVICE
INC.

SPECIAL NOTE

BASED ON A TOTALLY TRUE STORY was originally commissioned
by Geva Theatre Center, Rochester, New York.

Originally produced by Manhattan Theatre Club,
Lynne Meadow, Artistic Director; Barry Grove, Executive Producer,
on March 23, 2006.

Dedicated to Mark Blankenship, Warren Simons,
Harry and Mary Jane Ufland, and Howard Rosenstone

BASED ON A TOTALLY TRUE STORY was originally commissioned by Geva Theatre Center in Rochester, New York.

BASED ON A TOTALLY TRUE STORY received its world premiere at Center Stage II by Manhattan Theatre Club (Lynn Meadow, Artistic Director; Barry Grove, Executive Producer) in New York City on March 23, 2006. It was directed by Michael Bush; the set design was by Anna Louizos; the costume design was by Linda Cho; the lighting design was by Traci Klainer; the sound design was by Ryan Rumery; and the production stage manager was Gail Eve Malatesta. The cast was as follows:

ETHAN KEENE .... Carson Elrod
TYLER, APPLE BOY,
KIM'S GUY, HOT L.A. GUY .... Eric Heger
MARY ELLEN .... Kristine Neilsen
MICHAEL SULLIVAN .... Pedro Pascal
ETHAN'S DAD .... Michael Tucker

CHARACTERS

ETHAN KEENE, a playwright and comic book writer, late twenties

MICHAEL SULLIVAN, his boyfriend, also a writer in his late twenties, early thirties

TYLER, Ethan's editor at DC Comics, early thirties

MARY ELLEN, a movie producer in Hollywood, a woman in her late forties

APPLE BOY, works at the Apple Store in SoHo, hates his job

KIM'S GUY, works at Kim's Video Store on St. Marks, loves his job

ETHAN'S DAD, self-explanatory, in his fifties or early sixties

HOT L.A. GUY, trouble with a capital "T," is hot, lives in L.A., we hate him

One actor plays Ethan. One actor plays Michael. One actor plays Ethan's Dad. One actor plays Mary Ellen. One versatile actor plays Tyler, Apple Boy, Kim's Guy, and Hot L.A. Guy.

PLACE

Most of the play happens in New York. Various locations suggested minimally. Occasionally we cut to Los Angeles and Philadelphia, also suggested minimally.

TIME

The present, stretched out over two years.

BASED ON A TOTALLY TRUE STORY

ACT ONE

Theatrical limbo. Sudden spots on two young men, both in their twenties — Ethan and Michael — on opposite sides of the stage. Ethan, at least, wears glasses.

ETHAN. *(To audience.)* This is a story about a guy, a writer, and another guy, also a writer, and a dad (the first guy's dad), and a play the first guy wrote, and the people in Hollywood who want to turn that play into a movie, and what happens with the people in Hollywood, the first guy, the second guy, the first guy's dad, and what they learn about themselves and the world. *(Beat.)* It's a *slightly* familiar story, but that's okay because nobody likes things that are *too* original or challenging — *(Beat.)* — I eventually came to discover.

MICHAEL. Tell them about the play first, Ethan.

ETHAN. Right. *(To audience.)* The play I wrote. Is about a family. In crisis. There's a father, a marine biologist, and a mother, and their two boys, and a tragic boating accident, and one of the boys drowns, and the second boy *almost* drowns — (that's before the play starts) — and they live on a remote island off the coast of Newfoundland —

MICHAEL. *(To audience.)* Which is part of Canada.

ETHAN. *(To audience.)* Which means: It's cold, and dark, and miserable all the time, and basically this family is coming apart. The father ... becomes consumed by his work, the mother shuts down emotionally, stops going out, stops painting. (The mother's a painter; did I say that already?)

MICHAEL. Not yet.

ETHAN. *(To audience.)* Well, she is, and the surviving boy is brain-damaged because he was underwater for so long, he can't talk, he can't respond to things. *(Deep breath.)* And *then,* just as they're reaching a breaking point, this strange, hunky man washes up on the beach in front of their house and the family takes him in and weird things start to happen — good things, the boy's healed — but what the mother eventually realizes is that the strange, hunky man *isn't* a messenger of comfort, he's actually the ocean's herald of doom, sent to take the surviving son back into the ocean because he should've drowned with the first boy

MICHAEL. *(To audience.)* Which is what happens: The surviving son is dragged into the ocean — and drowns. The father is dragged into the ocean — and drowns. The mother's younger sister is dragged into the ocean — and drowns.

ETHAN. *(To audience.)* Actually, the strange, hunky guy snaps her neck — onstage — *then* drags her into the ocean.

MICHAEL. *(To audience.)* The only character who survives is the mother.

ETHAN. *(To audience.)* Who loses *everything* — her entire family — because they transgressed against nature —

MICHAEL. *(To audience.)* "Man Versus Nature" —

ETHAN. *(To audience.)* And she's left alone, and she's freezing, and she goes crazy. *(Beat.)* So, in other words, it's *not* a comedy.

MICHAEL. *(To audience.)* It's what they call in the entertainment world "a tough sell."

ETHAN. *(To audience.)* But whatever, it's a good play, with good characters, a good (if ultimately downbeat) story, so my agent sent it around, and a lot of theatres actually liked it.

MICHAEL. *(To audience.)* There were a lot of what entertainment people like to call "nibbles."

ETHAN. *(To audience.)* There were nibbles, and readings, and workshops — all of which went very, very well.

MICHAEL. *(To audience.)* And he, Ethan, my boyfriend, thought he was just the hottest shit *ever* —

ETHAN. — especially after producers from Hollywood called to tell me that … uhm … *(Ethan trails off.)*

MICHAEL. *(Reassuringly.)* It's all right — I'm all right with this.

ETHAN. I know, it just — *creeps* up on you, doesn't it?

MICHAEL. Just — take a deep breath and ease into it, Ethan, all right? And I'll — *(Mini-beat.)* — I'm gonna go, but I'll be back soon, okay?

ETHAN. Thanks, Michael. *(Michael exits. During this next speech, Ethan sets up a table and two chairs, sits down.)* So, my agent. Harold. Kept sending my play around — he even sent it to a couple of movie people, he said — and there were a lot of nibbles, a lot of first dates, but no one — no artistic director — could get beyond the fact that *both* of the kids in my play died. *(Beat.)* One dead kid is okay, apparently, but two dead kids is, like — what's *your* problem? *(Tyler, Ethan's editor — early thirties, from New York — enters carrying a sheaf of papers in his hands.)*

TYLER. Bro, this issue …

ETHAN. Yeah, Tyler? *(To audience, explaining.)* My day job — to support being a playwright — is writing *The Flash* for DC Comics.

TYLER. This issue, bro …

ETHAN. *(To audience.)* Tyler's my editor, he — edits me.

TYLER. I read it this morning on the subway …

ETHAN. And — how did it read?

TYLER. Effortlessly, bro. It's got *flow.*

ETHAN. Awesome.

TYLER. But you're gonna have to rewrite it.

ETHAN. *(To audience.)* Tyler's not bad for a straight guy who lives in, like, *Astoria,* but it does make things harder sometimes. *(Turns to Tyler.)* I am?

TYLER. You are. Because — the thing is — we got a mandate from corporate.

ETHAN. We did?

TYLER. They want — basically — for the Flash to tell his girlfriend that he's the Flash.

ETHAN. You mean reveal his secret identity?

TYLER. Essentially, yes.

ETHAN. You — "corporate" — want Wally West to tell his girlfriend Linda Parks that he's the Flash?

TYLER. In a nutshell. Because, they say, we have to somehow "deepen" his character.

ETHAN. But — but the Flash is the fastest man alive, Tyler. It's not in his nature to slow down, take stock of his life, open himself up —

TYLER. Not even to the woman he loves, bro?

ETHAN. *Especially* not to her.

TYLER. How come?

ETHAN. *Because,* Tyler — (and it's a little embarrassing that I have to explain this to you) — but it would make them both vulnerable. *(Beat.)* I mean, think about it: If their lives become so intertwined that Linda Parks knows everything about Wally West — including that he's the Flash — then his enemies can get to him through her. Like — they can hold her hostage and stuff.

TYLER. Yeah, okay, but look at this from the Flash's perspective —

ETHAN. That's all I *do,* Tyler. That's all I've *done* since — *(Beat.)* Growing up? All I wore was a Flash T-shirt. (Which actually wasn't even a T-shirt, it was a pajama top.) I drank from Flash tumblers, I played with Flash action figures, I had a Flash lunch box, there were Flash posters taped to my walls, up until two years ago I slept on Flash sheets —

TYLER. — All right — okay — I'll try talking to the higher-ups —

ETHAN. — Thank you.

TYLER. But I gotta warn you, they're pretty set on this direction.

ETHAN. Just — *try.*

TYLER. I will, bro. *(He stands to go. Slaps the sheaf of papers in his hands.)* Great work, by the way. Good flow. *(Tyler exits. Ethan takes out his laptop, opens it.)*

ETHAN. *(To audience.)* A list of places where I like to write and why: Doma, this tiny café in the Village that's always crowded, but it has the *best* tomato and bread soup *and* it's where John Cameron Mitchell likes to write. The Starbucks (I know) in the Barnes & Noble (I know) at Broadway and Sixty-sixth Street, because of that row of picture windows that look out over Lincoln Center (I know). *Annd* … where I am now: Java Boy, this place on Eighth Avenue, because I like their hot chocolate and they have free wireless (not because it's right in Chelsea and totally cruisy). *(Michael enters, carrying a cup of coffee. He approaches Ethan cautiously.)*

MICHAEL. Excuse me — Tim?

ETHAN. Who?

MICHAEL. Are you … Tim?

ETHAN. No, sorry, I'm —

MICHAEL. Oh, sorry, I thought you were —

ETHAN. — It's okay, I understand. *(Michael stands there for a few moments, not knowing what to do. He looks around the coffee shop, then:)*

MICHAEL. Actually, would it be all right if I — *(Looks around one last time.)* — could I join you?

ETHAN. Um — sure. Please.

MICHAEL. Thanks, thank you. *(Michael sits down.)* Is that a G4?

ETHAN. Pardon?

MICHAEL. Your laptop, is that a G4 or a — ?

ETHAN. Oh, yeah, no, it is. I just got it at the — uhm — at the Apple Store down in SoHo. Sort of an impulse purchase. I was having lunch at Balthazar with one of my friends and I'd just gotten this unexpected monster tax refund and I was originally only gonna buy an iPhone —

MICHAEL. How is it?

ETHAN. — Great, I love it. *(Beat.)* I actually just got it, so I'm still adjusting.

MICHAEL. You used to have a PC?

ETHAN. Yeah, exactly.

MICHAEL. Well, congratulations.

ETHAN. Yeah, I just got tired of seeing movies and everyone's always using an Apple, and I mean — I wanted to be special, too, you know?

MICHAEL. They're better machines, anyway. More — user-friendly.

ETHAN. Yeah, and if they break, you can take them down to the Apple Store — to the Genius Bar in the back — and one of those cute Apple *Boiz* will fix it for you while you wait.

MICHAEL. Uhm …

ETHAN. I actually have no idea why I said that, so please just feel free to, you know — ignore —

MICHAEL. Are you a writer?

ETHAN. Uhm …

MICHAEL. Because it looks — it looked, while I was getting my coffee — like you were actually writing. Your lips were moving, you were gesturing to yourself —

ETHAN. *I* was?

MICHAEL. It looked like you were having a very intense conversation with yourself.

ETHAN. *(Incredibly mortified.)* (Oh, God …)

MICHAEL. No, no, you looked — it was very endearing, actually.

ETHAN. I am so incredibly mortified right now, you have no idea.

MICHAEL. Don't be; it was — very cute, actually.

ETHAN. No, it's actually a sign of dementia, you know, talking to yourself, and —

MICHAEL. I do it all the time.

ETHAN. Now you're just trying to make me feel better —

MICHAEL. No, I'm trying to make you think I'm charming.

11

ETHAN. Oh. *(Beat.)* Wait, what?

MICHAEL. My name's Michael Sullivan.

ETHAN. Ethan. Keene. *(They shake.)*

MICHAEL. So, Ethan, are you a writer?

ETHAN. A playwright. And I write comic books, too.

MICHAEL. You mean like *Superman*?

ETHAN. Well, *The Flash*.

MICHAEL. The Flash is the one who … does something with lightning bolts?

ETHAN. Runs really fast, actually. *(Quick beat.)* Which — *but* — he *does* have a lightning bolt on his chest — it's his chest insignia — so maybe that's what you were thinking of. Maybe. Possibly. *(Awkward beat. Michael and Ethan smile at each other.)* Anyway …

MICHAEL. Michael.

ETHAN. Anyway, Michael … *(Hating it but whatever:)* What do *you* do?

MICHAEL. I'm a writer, too.

ETHAN. *(To audience.)* And we were off. A movie date at Film Forum the weekend after we met —

MICHAEL. *(To audience.)* His choice, not mine.

ETHAN. *(To audience.)* — The 1959 French horror movie *Eyes Without a Face* —

MICHAEL. Followed by dinner at Orso on West Forty-sixth Street the week after that.

ETHAN. Followed by a Michael Cunningham reading at the Barnes & Noble on Twenty-third Street (can you *bear* it?)

MICHAEL. Followed by a disturbing Neil LaBute play at the Public —

ETHAN. Followed by a Scissor Sisters concert at Irving Plaza —

MICHAEL. Cute e-mailing back-and-forth throughout —

ETHAN. Culminating (a month and seven dates after our first meeting) with the following e-mail:

MICHAEL. "Hey, sexy, bring your toothbrush and pajamas tonight, okay? You're staying over. Smiley face." *(Bling noise!)*

ETHAN. *(To audience.)* I mean, can you *bear* it?

MICHAEL. *(To audience.)* Not that there weren't problems —

ETHAN. *Challenges,* sweetie. *Opportunities.*

MICHAEL. *(To audience.)* Two writers, you understand …

ETHAN. *(To audience.)* A playwright — me — and a staff writer for *The Voice*.

MICHAEL. *(To audience.)* A cultural *critic* for *The Voice.*

ETHAN. *(To audience.)* But, you know, whatever, Michael liked cute, nerdy guys, I liked — anybody who liked cute, nerdy guys, he was smart —

MICHAEL. *(To audience.)* — *He* was smart —

ETHAN. *(Pleased, to audience.)* — We were *both* smart. And the sex — *(Quick beat, big smile.)* — I have to say the sex was pretty —

MICHAEL. — The sex was great.

ETHAN. And — *(Quick aside to Michael, agreeing.)* — it was, yes — *(Back to audience.)* — but we also had a lot in common.

MICHAEL. *(To audience.)* Subscriptions to *The New York Observer* —

ETHAN. *(To audience.)* — gym memberships at Equinox neither of us really use —

MICHAEL. *(To audience.)* — celebrity crushes on both Rachel Ray and Anderson Cooper —

ETHAN. *(To audience.)* — pathological fear of circuses in general and Cirque du Soleil in particular —

MICHAEL. *(To audience.)* — so against the odds (and by odds, I mean the odds of two semi-complex, fairly attractive, overly literate gay men meeting in New York City and *not* immediately going to bed), we started dating.

ETHAN. Successfully.

MICHAEL. *Semi*-successfully.

ETHAN. *(To audience.)* And the writing — Michael's reviews, his profiles, his novel-in-progress —

MICHAEL. *(To audience.)* — Ethan's plays and comic books —

ETHAN. *(To audience.)* — rarely, if ever, got in the way. *(Beat, to Michael.)* I mean, certainly my *playwriting* wasn't an issue, since I didn't work on a single play while —

MICHAEL. *(To audience.)* Until that phone call from his producers — *(A cell phone in Ethan's bag starts to ring. And ring.)*

ETHAN. You know, Michael, I don't *have* to take it. I can just … let it go into voice-mail.

MICHAEL. Take it? Ethan, you *took* it. You *always* took it. *(Smiles, shakes his head ruefully.)* You remember your exact words — what you said — that day? *(Ethan pulls the cell phone out of his bag, checks it, silences it.)*

ETHAN. "Oh, sweetie, it's a 310 area-code, it could be those movie people who read my play, I should take this, do you mind?"

MICHAEL. Not at all, sweetie, I gotta go anyway, I'm interviewing Joyce Carol Oates.

ETHAN. What, did she write *another* book?

MICHAEL. Yes, I told you already.

ETHAN. You did?

MICHAEL. Yes, and you told me to tell her that she needs to slow down. That a person can't write and publish three books a year for the last twenty years without the overall quality of her work suffering.

ETHAN. *I* said that?

MICHAEL. Do you *ever* listen when we talk?

ETHAN. Michael ...

MICHAEL. You just put that on vibrate, didn't you? *(Michael exits, kissing Ethan quickly.)*

ETHAN. *(To audience.)* So — uhm — three months into my relationship with Michael, the same week we move in together (I know — crazy!), I answer my ringing cell phone and it's — *(Quick spot on Mary Ellen. She and Ethan are talking on the phone.)*

MARY ELLEN. Ethan, hi, I'm Mary Ellen Eustice, my husband is Barry Eustice, you'll talk to him later, I'm the one who works with writers, how are you?

ETHAN. Uhm — good.

MARY ELLEN. First of all, I have to tell you, your agent — when he sent us your play — said that you write *The Flash* comic book, is that true?

ETHAN. Oh, yeah, I do.

MARY ELLEN. I have to tell you — my son, Tommy, *loves The Flash* comic book, are you connected at all to the movie?

ETHAN. They're making a *Flash* movie?

MARY ELLEN. Starring Orlando Bloom, who can't open a movie, I don't think — but the girls, the teeny-boppers, love him, so what can you do?

ETHAN. Yeah, my sister thinks he's totally hot.

MARY ELLEN. Yes, well, at any rate, your agent sent us your play —

ETHAN. Yeah, Harold told me you might be call —

MARY ELLEN. — and we love it.

ETHAN. You do?

MARY ELLEN. We think we can sell it *and* get it made.

ETHAN. My play — would be a movie?

MARY ELLEN. We think there's the potential for that, yes, Barry and I believe. *(Beat.)* It's very cinematic, have people told you that?

ETHAN. Yeah, but — I mean — not as a compliment.

MARY ELLEN. Now we can go about this two ways, Ethan. We can try to sell your play to a studio and then *they'll* assign a writer to it. *Or* you could write the screenplay yourself and then we'll try to sell *that.* Which were you thinking?

ETHAN. I mean, I wasn't, really.

MARY ELLEN. Oh, come on. You're a *person,* aren't you?

ETHAN. I — *(Confused.)* — what?

MARY ELLEN. Oh, Ethan, you're going to tell me that you've *never* thought about turning your play into a movie for, say, Nicole Kidman?

ETHAN. I *love* Nicole Kidman.

MARY ELLEN. Me, too, but she did *The Others,* so she may not want to make this kind of movie again.

ETHAN. Yeah, but — my movie's way better than that.

MARY ELLEN. Well, yes, but you don't actually have a movie yet, you have a play, and potential, and *me.*

ETHAN. Nicole Kidman doesn't want to make my movie?

MARY ELLEN. Potentially she doesn't. You have to write it first. Or we can try to sell your play and someone else can write it.

ETHAN. No way. No one else is writing my movie.

MARY ELLEN. I agree completely and here's why: This story is yours, Ethan. It means something to you. You had an impulse, a spark, something inspired you, and then — then this play came out. This beautiful, dark, haunting, strange, *wonderful* play just — it just *emerged,* didn't it? *(Before Ethan can answer.)* At least that's what it feels like, though I'm sure you *agonized* over it, writing and rewriting it and shaping it and turning it into this — this miracle, Ethan, because that's what it is. Because I've read a lot of plays, Ethan, but yours — yours is *different.* It's *special.* It has *potential.* And more, it has a *movie* inside it. And not just a movie, a *commercial* movie, which makes it the best kind of play.

ETHAN. *(Overcome, almost crying.)* I ... Mary Ellen ... Thank you.

MARY ELLEN. And I want you to put as much of that first impulse, that initial spark into the screenplay version of your play. Because — and this is the sad, horrible, soul-crushing truth about writing movies, Ethan — eventually? A director will become attached to your screenplay. And he — maybe she, but probably he (men!) — will start to give you notes. And you will have to *incorporate* them. And your screenplay will get further and further away from that impulse — spark — whatever — that first moved you to put fingers to keyboard.

ETHAN. *(Cosmic outrage.)* That is so — *wrong.*

MARY ELLEN. I agree. *(Beat.)* So the more *you* you put in your screenplay, the more *you* there will be when we all come out at the other end — if you follow me.

ETHAN. I do, but — I mean — I'm sure Harold told you that I've never written a screenplay.

MARY ELLEN. Doesn't matter. Do you know Structure?

ETHAN. Yes.

MARY ELLEN. Do you know Character?

ETHAN. Yes.

MARY ELLEN. Do you know Story?

ETHAN. Uh …

MARY ELLEN. You know Story; a person doesn't write the play you wrote without knowing Story. (You may not know you know Story, but believe me, you know Story.)

ETHAN. I guess I do, yeah …

MARY ELLEN. Then you can write a movie.

ETHAN. Yes — *(Realizes.)* — *yes!*

MARY ELLEN. So — write a movie, Ethan.

ETHAN. I will.

MARY ELLEN. Great. *(Beat.)* Now before you get started, can I put *one* tiny, little bug in your ear?

ETHAN. Sure.

MARY ELLEN. Do both of the kids *have* to die? Speaking to you as a mother, it feels *excessive.*

ETHAN. Well — I mean — that's the whole point …

MARY ELLEN. Yes, but can I tell you a story? *(Before Ethan answers.)* Stephen King — you know Stephen King —

ETHAN. I'm familiar with Stephen King.

MARY ELLEN. Well, then, you must know Cujo, the killer dog? A mother and her son are trapped in a car and they're terrorized by this enormous rabid St. Bernard? Foam? Fangs? Flies?

ETHAN. Sure.

MARY ELLEN. And in the book, the kid dies.

ETHAN. Because, Stephen King said, that was the right ending.

MARY ELLEN. I agree — completely — for the novel. Who am I to tell Mr. King he's wrong? *(Beat.)* But in the movie version of *Cujo,* the kid lives and the mother impales the killer dog with a broken-off baseball bat, and you know what?

ETHAN. *That* was the right ending?

MARY ELLEN. For the movie, absolutely. And you know who decided that?

ETHAN. Stephen King?

MARY ELLEN. Because he *knew.*

ETHAN. He — ? *(Takes this in, decides:)* Okay, fine. The little boy from my play can live.

MARY ELLEN. Really? *(Beat.)* I mean, don't get me wrong, I'm *thrilled,* this means we can do business, but somehow I was expecting more *resistance.*

ETHAN. Yes — well — but what you don't know is? A month ago? I wrote an issue of *The Flash* in which Wally West actually confesses to his girlfriend that he's the Flash. *(Beat.)* And anyway, we're talking about a movie, not my play. And the second kid dies in my play because *that's* the right ending — for the play. *(Beat.)* But this movie — when I write it — this movie will be … a movie.

MARY ELLEN. Agreed.

ETHAN. And I love the movies, I do, I grew up going to the movies with my dad —

MARY ELLEN. I *love* your father; God *bless* your father!

ETHAN. — And I know you serve different gods when you write a movie.

MARY ELLEN. Dark gods, Ethan.

ETHAN. And I'm … okay with that. Because my play's never gonna get produced, I don't think, but I want this movie — if I'm gonna write it — I want it to get *made.* So — where's the dotted line? Screenplay for immortal soul? I'll sign.

MARY ELLEN. You're precious, you know that? You're like F. Scott Fitzgerald when he first went to Hollywood — *before* his crack-up.

ETHAN. Okay, well — I guess I'll start tonight.

MARY ELLEN. Great — *(Mini-beat.)* — just two more things but they're *tiny. (Quickly.)* Your play is set in Newfoundland, which is — if I'm not mistaken — in Canada?

ETHAN. It is.

MARY ELLEN. Yes, well, your movie needs to be set in the United States, in America, no one likes Canada, no one knows where it is, *what* it is, is it part of Europe, who knows?

ETHAN. But the cold, the snow, they're so important to the story —

MARY ELLEN. No, no, we *love* the cold and snow — *(Mini-beat.)* — it just can't be *Canadian* cold and snow.

ETHAN. Okay, but then where — ?

MARY ELLEN. How about Maine? (Stephen King lives in Maine.) Have you ever been to Maine?

ETHAN. No.

MARY ELLEN. Oh, you have to go. Barry and I have a house there, we'll have you up, but let me tell you: It gets very, very cold in Maine, Ethan. And it snows — snows A LOT, in fact. And there are islands, dozens and dozens of little, creepy islands you could set your movie on.

ETHAN. Off the coast of Maine?

MARY ELLEN. Oh, God, it's so terrifying, isn't it, just those words — "an isolated island off the coast of Maine" — I'm scared already.

ETHAN. But, I mean — I read *Variety*, I watch *Entertainment Tonight* — won't my movie most likely be *shot* in Canada?

MARY ELLEN. Ironic, isn't it? *(Short pause as Ethan considers this. Then:)*

ETHAN. Okay, I can do that, too. *Poof*, it's done. My family now lives on an island off the coast of Maine.

MARY ELLEN. An *isolated* island; it's got to be remote, Ethan, the edge of the world!

ETHAN. Yeah, but is Maine really considered — ?

MARY ELLEN. The second thing —

ETHAN. Yes?

MARY ELLEN. Absolutely tiny — a speck, a fleck, an atom, *nothing* — but now I have to talk to you as a producer, I have to put on my producing hat and tell you that right now, in Hollywood, there is a huge demand for these kinds of movies. Grown-up, semi-sophisticated horror movies. *What Lies Beneath*, *The Others*, *The Ring*, *The Ring 2* —

ETHAN. *The Ring* movies are sophisticated?

MARY ELLEN. Even better, Ethan, they're *Asian* — *(Mini-beat.)* — but you see what I'm saying?

ETHAN. I think, yeah —

MARY ELLEN. There's a window right now — a *market* for the kind of movie your play wants to be.

ETHAN. Wow.

MARY ELLEN. But we have to strike while the iron's hot! Which means *you* — you have to write, and write *fast!*

ETHAN. Fast?

MARY ELLEN. Like a *bunny,* Ethan — no, no — like the Flash. *(Beat.)* And I know you have other commitments, I know you have *serious* plays to write, I know you have a life, but Ethan?

ETHAN. Yes?

MARY ELLEN. This is the *movies,* Ethan, if you — *comprendez-moi?*

ETHAN. I ... I *think* I do, Mary Ellen.

MARY ELLEN. So write us a movie!

ETHAN. I will.

MARY ELLEN. Good — *(Beat.)* — call us if you need help, we're here, Barry, as well, but always try me first.

ETHAN. Oh — *(Mary Ellen hangs up.)* — kay. *(Pleased with himself, Ethan calls Michael, who is out and about.)*

MICHAEL. Hey, cutie, I'm just leaving the office right now —

ETHAN. Okay, who has the coolest boyfriend maybe ever?

MICHAEL. Uhhhh — that would be you.

ETHAN. Or would it be the guy who's dating the guy who is, as of ten seconds ago, writing a movie for Nicole Kidman.

MICHAEL. *You're writing a movie for Nicole Kidman?*

ETHAN. Well — maybe, hopefully, I don't know, Mary Ellen thinks it's possible.

MICHAEL. Who's Mary Ellen?

ETHAN. Hel-*lo,* my producer!

MICHAEL. Okay, sweetie? We actually *don't* share the same brain, so you're gonna have to explain this to me like I'm a second-grader.

ETHAN. Which I will do on the subway, on the way.

MICHAEL. On the way to...? *(The lights change and we are in:)*

ETHAN. I *love* the Apple Store!

MICHAEL. You know what we should do? We should celebrate!

ETHAN. Absolutely —

MICHAEL. A nice, quiet, romantic dinner at ... I don't know, Chevy's? *(But they are approaching an employee of the Apple Store: Apple Boy.)*

ETHAN. We will, sweetie, I swear, but right now — *(To the Apple Boy.)* Hi, how are you? I need to get ... uh, what's that program so you can write screenplays?

APPLE BOY. Final Draft 7, sir.

ETHAN. Yeah, Final Draft 7, right. Do you have Final Draft 7 for Macs?

APPLE BOY. This is the Apple Store, sir. All we have is Final Draft for Macs.

ETHAN. Awesome, can I get one? I'm a writing a screenplay!

APPLE BOY. *Really.*

ETHAN. My first one!

APPLE BOY. Fascinating.

MICHAEL. Excuse me, but are you — wait — you're *judging* my boyfriend right now, aren't you?

APPLE BOY. Silently, yes.

MICHAEL. Yeah, I thought so. Listen — *(Checks his name tag.)* — Roger — I appreciate the fact that probably a lot of pretentious writer-types come into your store, and ask for Final Draft, and act condescendingly towards you — which must really bother you — (The way people writing on laptops in coffee shops really bothers you, too, I'm sure.) —

APPLE BOY. At Java Boy on Eighth Avenue, especially, yes.

MICHAEL. Yes — well — but some of those people? They actually *are* writers, okay? Who write for a living. Who write because they have to. Because there is something *burning* inside them. Who write because they see something in the world other people *don't* see.

ETHAN. Sweetie —

MICHAEL. And they're struggling, most of them. They've made sacrifices. They have student loans.

ETHAN. Okay, now this is really TMI —

MICHAEL. And this man right here — *(Meaning Ethan.)* — this beautiful, awkward, slightly neurotic man (who hates that I'm doing this right now) — is one of those people. A writer. Who actually writes things. Plays — many of which have been produced —

APPLE BOY. In New York?

MICHAEL. *Soon* in New York — *(Mini-beat.)* — not that New York is the end-all, be-all for emerging playwrights —

ETHAN. Uhm, sweetie, it actually, kind of —

MICHAEL. — and not just plays, but comic books, too, about super heroes —

APPLE BOY. Superman?

MICHAEL. No.

APPLE BOY. Batman?

MICHAEL. Not yet.

APPLE BOY. Wonder Woman?

ETHAN. The Flash, it's the Flash.

APPLE BOY. The *who?*

MICHAEL. — Plays, comic books, and now a screenplay. Which is why we're here, buying Final Draft 7.

ETHAN. And maybe an iPhone; they're so darn sleek and sexy —

MICHAEL. So whatever frustrated ambition you're sublimating here … put it in your journal, all right? Because all *we* want is this overpriced software — *(Beat.)* — *please. (Short pause.)*

APPLE BOY. One moment, and I'll bring it out to you.

MICHAEL. I would really appreciate that, thank you. *(He goes. Ethan turns to Michael.)*

ETHAN. Michael … *(Realizing it.)* You just, like, totally just defended me.

MICHAEL. Yes.

ETHAN. You're, like, totally my hero right now.

MICHAEL. Which makes you, what, my sidekick? My teenage ward?

ETHAN. You know, Michael, a big reason for why I'm doing this is us. I mean, the amount of money a screenplay can potentially bring in is, like, *huge,* sweetie.

MICHAEL. I'm … well aware.

ETHAN. Enough that we could quit our day jobs and — and just write.

MICHAEL. That would be — very nice.

ETHAN. Cool, so — one more stop, 'kay? *(The lights change. Now we're in:)*

MICHAEL. Oh, come on, *Kim's?*

ETHAN. *(To audience.)* Down on St. Mark's Place. *Literally* the greatest video store in the world. *(Michael and Ethan are making their way to the Kim's Guy, standing in one of the store's aisles.)* Hi, how are you? Do you have a — uhm — an Asian horror movie section? You know, Japanese horror?

KIM'S GUY. Pre- or post-1971?

MICHAEL. There's a difference?

ETHAN. Sweetie, please. *(To Kim's Guy.)* Post- would be great.

KIM'S GUY. What titles in particular?

ETHAN. Oh, God, I'm not sure, I'm looking for … subtle, sophisticated, understated horror … Families in crises, mothers protecting their children from supernatural menaces …

MICHAEL. This is absurd. Like they're actually going to have —

KIM'S GUY. Well, there's *Ringu,* of course, and *Ringu 2.* And *Ju-On,* and *Ju-On 2.* And *Uzumaki,* and *Dark Water,* and *The Imp.* And …

Premonition, and *The Pulse*, and *The Eye*, and …

ETHAN. Yes?

KIM'S GUY. … Actually, that'll be enough to get you started.

ETHAN. Great, I'll take them.

KIM'S GUY. One moment, I'll be right back. *(The Kim's Guy goes and Michael looks at Ethan.)*

MICHAEL. You'll take them? All of them? Do you even *like* Asian horror movies?

ETHAN. They're research. You wouldn't know — you're not in the industry — but Asian horror, J horror, is very big in Hollywood right now. They're — they're an investment.

MICHAEL. They're twenty-five dollars each, is what they are.

ETHAN. You know, I don't think I've told you recently …

MICHAEL. I know.

ETHAN. I do, you know. *(Michael and Ethan smile at each other.)*

MICHAEL. So can we go home?

ETHAN. Anything you want. *(Sound and lights and the way Ethan and Michael hold their right hands in the air, indicate that we're on a New York City subway car now.)*

MICHAEL. So you write this movie, and — before the millions start rolling in, of course — what happens with your comic book writing?

ETHAN. What do you mean?

MICHAEL. I mean, will you have time to write *The Flash* —

ETHAN. I *love* writing *The Flash* —

MICHAEL. All right, but what about the new play you've been talking about wanting to — no, no, no, *needing* to write? As an artist — no, no, no, as a *citizen of the world?*

ETHAN. Uhm, that's why God made backburners, Michael. I mean, this is the *movies.*

MICHAEL. All right, but what about being a loving, giving, emotionally available boyfriend?

ETHAN. Michael. You write for *The Voice* and are always working on your novel, and *I'm* totally supportive, aren't I?

MICHAEL. Well, you're certainly always *telling* me you are. *(Short pause.)*

ETHAN. … Is everything okay, Michael?

MICHAEL. I know I didn't get a phone call from Hollywood, Ethan, I know no one's throwing enormous amounts of money at me —

ETHAN. *Potentially* enormous amounts of —

MICHAEL. — but I actually *did* have a day today. Things — stuff — *did* actually happen to me.

ETHAN. *(Realizing.)* Joyce Carol Oates, and I didn't ask about your interview with her ...

MICHAEL. No, Ethan.

ETHAN. I'm *so* — *(Beat.)* — how was it? Was she — ?

MICHAEL. Fine, she was fine. *(Beat.)* Really nice, actually. *(Beat.)* I mean, for someone who writes forty-two novels a year.

ETHAN. I know. In the time we've been here talking, she's probably written, like, *a novella.*

MICHAEL. I asked her how she's able to do it — write so much — and she said: "How? A better question, don't you think, is *why* I write so much."

ETHAN. Oh, that's good —

MICHAEL. *(Suddenly.)* I don't want to feel this way, Ethan.

ETHAN. No, and you shouldn't. I mean — *I* shouldn't make you feel that way — if I am. If I do. (Do I?) And, uhm, what way are we talking about exactly?

MICHAEL. I'm *not* needy. And ... I don't want to be the *second* most important thing in anybody's life.

ETHAN. Of course not. *(Beat.)* Michael ...

MICHAEL. It's okay, I know our careers aren't always going to be in sync —

ETHAN. No, that's not ... I was going to say ... *(Searches for it.)* You're like my ... Linda Parks.

MICHAEL. The Flash's girlfriend?

ETHAN. Because — no, listen — because she's the most important thing in his life. Because no matter what happens to him — no matter what Gorilla Grodd throws at him — even when he gets lost in time — he *always* comes back to her. He gets on his cosmic treadmill and fights through *whatever* to reach her. *(Short pause.)* She *anchors* him. Makes him, you know — human.

MICHAEL. I make you human, Ethan?

ETHAN. You do. *(Beat.)* So actually ...

MICHAEL. ... *you're* the one who's needy?

ETHAN. I mean, if one of us *has* to be needy ... *(Light change, Ethan and Michael stand, and now we're in their apartment.)*

MICHAEL. Check messages; I'll get menus —

ETHAN. Menus? I thought we were ordering from Better Burger?

(Michael goes and Ethan hits a button on the answering machine. A spot on Ethan's Dad, in his living room in Philadelphia.)

ETHAN'S DAD. Hello, Ethan and Michael, this message is for Ethan. It's your dad, calling to remind you that it's my birthday in two and a half weeks —

ETHAN. I remembered.

ETHAN'S DAD. — and that you promised to come down for my party —

ETHAN. Wait, is that *this* month?

ETHAN'S DAD. — so go ahead and buy your ticket on Amtrak, and Mom and I will reimburse you when you get here —

ETHAN. No, you won't.

ETHAN'S DAD. — so call us to confirm, please, or e-mail us …

ETHAN. *(To audience.)* This is where my dad shows how *evolved* he is.

ETHAN'S DAD. … and please — give our best to Michael. *(The machine clicks off, the spot on Ethan's Dad goes out, and Michael reenters.)*

MICHAEL. Okay, so I ordered us Better Chicken Burgers, Better Baked Fries, and Better Smoothies.

ETHAN. Hey, so my mom and dad send you their better best.

MICHAEL. Oh, good, I send them my best, too.

ETHAN. Michael …

MICHAEL. Well — I mean — really, Ethan.

ETHAN. Okay, okay …

MICHAEL. They're very nice people. And — you know — one day I hope to meet them.

ETHAN. You've met them.

MICHAEL. Get to know them, then.

ETHAN. They're my parents, Michael, *I* don't even know them.

MICHAEL. Well, were they calling to remind you it's your father's sixtieth birthday in two weeks?

ETHAN. Yeah, but — wait, how did you know?

MICHAEL. It's circled on your *Flash* calendar in the kitchen. *(Lights change. Michael exits and Ethan talks to the audience.)*

ETHAN. Okay — so: two weeks of trying to figure out how to use Final Draft 7 — two weeks of forcing Michael to watch Asian horror movies with me — two weeks of burning the midnight oil because *The Flash* is double-shipping next month — two weeks of writing and rewriting and cutting — I finish the first twenty-five pages of my screenplay, which I send off to Mary Ellen the same day I hop the Amtrak to visit my mom and dad in Philly. *(Spot on Ethan's Dad, waiting for him at the train station in Philadelphia.)* My dad meets me at the station — announces:

ETHAN'S DAD. We're going to Sears! *(And that's where we are now, browsing in Sears' tool department.)* They don't have a Sears in New York, do they? In the city?

ETHAN. Uhm — not that I'm aware of, Dad.

ETHAN'S DAD. Where do you shop, then?

ETHAN. What do you mean?

ETHAN'S DAD. For tools — where do you get your tools? *(Ethan just looks at his dad.)* What do you do when you have household repairs?

ETHAN. Call the super. *(Beat.)* Or, you know, Michael does them.

ETHAN'S DAD. He does?

ETHAN. Oh, yeah, he's very — he's a handy guy.

ETHAN'S DAD. You're doing well, then, the two of you?

ETHAN. Oh, yeah, we're fine.

ETHAN'S DAD. He *does* know he's always welcome here, I hope.

ETHAN. Of course he knows, Dad. He's just ... busy with his writing, his novel and stuff ... *(Beat.)* He sends his regards, though.

ETHAN'S DAD. Uh-huh. And how's your screenplay coming along?

ETHAN. I don't know, I just sent off the first chunk, we'll see.

ETHAN'S DAD. What about your playwriting? You're still keeping up with it? Because remember —

ETHAN. — Yeah, it's all under control, Dad, and — uhm — what's with the third-degree? Why are we at Sears, anyway? You only ever brought me here when we needed to have a "very special talk," away ... from ... the ... *(Realizes.)* Is everything okay, dad?

ETHAN'S DAD. We've never been an overly ... *demonstrative* family, have we? Not much for ... sharing and the like?

ETHAN. I guess ... not really, no.

ETHAN'S DAD. But you were happy, weren't you? Growing up? You had a good childhood?

ETHAN. Of course not, but I wear that as a badge of honor.

ETHAN'S DAD. Your mom and I ... we were good to you? Supportive of you? And your brother and your sister?

ETHAN. Dad ...

ETHAN'S DAD. You don't have any regrets? And resentments

towards us? Your mom and me?

ETHAN. Dad, what's — ?

ETHAN'S DAD. Ethan, I don't think I love your mom anymore. *(Short pause.)* I love — I'm *in* love with — someone else.

ETHAN. Oh, come on, of course you're not.

ETHAN'S DAD. Ethan, I am. With a woman who loves me and —

ETHAN. *Mom* loves you, you love Mom —

ETHAN'S DAD. I don't — she doesn't.

ETHAN. *(This sinks in, then:)* Did Mom tell you that?

ETHAN'S DAD. No.

ETHAN. Okay, so then it's total speculation on your part?

ETHAN'S DAD. However your mom feels about me —

ETHAN. — *You* don't love *her?*

ETHAN'S DAD. — No.

ETHAN. Seriously?

ETHAN'S DAD. Not for — years, Eath.

ETHAN. Well, Jesus, Dad, this is — I mean, it's kind of a bomb.

ETHAN'S DAD. I know.

ETHAN. Jesus, what does Mom say?

ETHAN'S DAD. I haven't discussed it with her yet. *(Beat, then:)*

ETHAN. *What?*

ETHAN'S DAD. I don't want her getting upset for no good reason.

ETHAN. Uhm, her marriage falling apart is actually a *very* good reason, Dad. *(Beat.)* Jesus, who *does* know?

ETHAN'S DAD. Me … my friend, obviously …

ETHAN. Your "friend" — wow, *euphemism* much?

ETHAN'S DAD. … and now you.

ETHAN. Oh, come *on,* Dad!

ETHAN'S DAD. I had to tell someone. You and your brother made the most sense —

ETHAN. And naturally you chose me. Because when it comes to deep, dark, dirty secrets —

ETHAN'S DAD. I flipped a coin. *(Beat.)*

ETHAN. Wait, really?

ETHAN'S DAD. But then, when it came up heads, I thought maybe you could help us figure out what our next step should be. (The writer's mind, always problem-solving …) If we should stay here in Philadelphia, if we should ask the bank for a joint-transfer to another city —

ETHAN. Oh, you work together — *that's* how you met?

ETHAN'S DAD. I didn't go looking for this, Ethan. And I hope you believe me when I tell you that I didn't do this to hurt anyone —

ETHAN. You have to tell Mom, Dad.

ETHAN'S DAD. I know. And Janice knows she needs to tell her husband —

ETHAN. *WHAT?! SHE'S MARRIED, TOO?*

ETHAN'S DAD. Almost twenty-five years.

ETHAN. Oh, well, that's a relief, because now we know that at least you're *BOTH* insane!

ETHAN'S DAD. I'll tell your mom, Ethan, as soon as the rest … gets sorted. *(Beat.)* In the meantime … Why don't you chew on what I've just told you, see if there are any insights you can offer me, and we'll go home and pretend we didn't have this conversation, all right?

ETHAN. Oh … kay …

ETHAN'S DAD. Thanks, thank you, Son. *(Ethan and his dad hug, then Ethan's Dad exits. Ethan pulls out his cell phone, dials. Spot on Michael, at a desk with his open laptop. He answers his ringing phone.)*

MICHAEL'S VOICE. — This is Michael.

ETHAN. Hi …

MICHAEL. Hi!

ETHAN. What are you doing?

MICHAEL. Working. Where are you?

ETHAN. Oh, you know … standing in the tool department at Sears.

MICHAEL. Wow, there is so much about that statement that chills me.

ETHAN. Listen, are you *Voice*-Working or Working-on-Your-Novel-Working?

MICHAEL. Uh, pretending to be *Voice*-Working but really Working-on-My-Novel-Working. I just finished —

ETHAN. — Michael, there's nothing … *weird* between us right now, is there?

MICHAEL. Define weird.

ETHAN. Nothing … you're wondering about or maybe want to tell me?

MICHAEL. Sweetie, I have no idea what you're talking —

ETHAN. *Distance,* Michael, have you noticed any *distance* between us?

MICHAEL. You mean like emotional — ?

ETHAN. *Yes!* For God's sake, *yes* — that's *exactly* what I —

MICHAEL. — Of course I haven't.

ETHAN. Okay, but if you did feel it — or if there were something else wrong between us — we would talk about it, right? You wouldn't just, like, *desert* me, would you?

MICHAEL. Of course I wouldn't.

ETHAN. Do you promise?

MICHAEL. Ethan … what's happening? Are you — ?

ETHAN. I'm fine, I'm just being all … weird and paranoid and needy.

MICHAEL. Ethan …

ETHAN. Mostly I was just calling 'cause I missed you …

MICHAEL. Well … I miss you, too.

ETHAN. I … I'm really crazy about you, Michael.

MICHAEL. Me, too.

ETHAN. Oh-kay, well —

MICHAEL. — And oh, before I forget, those producers called. *(Short pause.)*

ETHAN. *My* producers?

MICHAEL. They said call them back at your earliest — *(Lights shift. Ethan is now talking to Mary Ellen — Michael remains on stage.)*

ETHAN. — Mary Ellen, hi, it's me, I'm so sorry it's taken me so long to get back to you, I just got your message from my boyfriend, who's not in the industry and therefore doesn't understand how time-sensitive —

MARY ELLEN. It's fine, really.

ETHAN. No, there's no excuse, and as soon as I get back to New York —

MARY ELLEN. Ethan, it's fine, the important thing is that Barry and I read the pages you sent us —

ETHAN. Yes, and?

MARY ELLEN. — And we loveloveLOVE them. Really, they're just great. We think you've done a great job of opening up the story, of moving it along, of making the characters likable —

ETHAN. — Yeah, I really wanted to make the husband more sympathetic than he is in the play —

MARY ELLEN. — Oh, and it reads, we absolutely get that —

ETHAN. — Oh great —

MARY ELLEN. — But: a couple of things.

ETHAN. — Oh?

MARY ELLEN. No, no — *minor* things. *Nothing* things. *(Quick beat.)* Your opening?

28

ETHAN. Yeah?

MARY ELLEN. Needs to be scary. *(Beat.)* Right now, it's just the mom and the dad and their deaf-mute son on the beach, and they're not really doing anything, are they?

ETHAN. Well — I mean — talking …

MARY ELLEN. So Barry and I were thinking: What if we add jellyfish? Because what's scarier than jellyfish?

ETHAN. Uhm…?

MARY ELLEN. You're swimming in the ocean, you're almost completely naked, you're vulnerable, you're thinking of *Jaws*, you've just hit a cold spot, and all of a sudden you feel it —

ETHAN. A …

MARY ELLEN. — A jellyfish's clammy, squishy, *pulsating* body brushing across your bare stomach.

ETHAN. My …

MARY ELLEN. Scary, right? In a primal scary way? *(Before Ethan can respond.)* So Barry and I were thinking: Cut the family talking — get them into the ocean (or start with them in the ocean, maybe that's better) — and have them be attacked —

ETHAN. — by a jellyfish?

MARY ELLEN. *Hundreds* of jellyfish, Ethan — we'll computer-generate them! If one jellyfish is scary, a swarm of them is terrifying.

ETHAN. Okay, but —

MARY ELLEN. Try it, see what happens.

ETHAN. — Okay.

MARY ELLEN. And in the meantime, I'm gonna e-mail you a couple of other notes, but the important thing is — get that opening right and keep pushing forward. Barry and I were talking to a couple of directors — a couple of very big, very big-time directors — and they were very, very responsive —

ETHAN. Really?

MARY ELLEN. — So keep writing and call if you have any questions. Me or Barry, but try me first, okay? *(Mary Ellen clicks off and exits, and Ethan turns — sheepishly — to Michael, who turns to the audience.)*

MICHAEL. *(To audience.)* So Ethan cut his trip short and came back to New York —

ETHAN. — Hi.

MICHAEL. Anything wrong?

ETHAN. Nothing, I just got — restless.

MICHAEL. But what about your dad's birthday?

ETHAN. We celebrated early, a day early.

MICHAEL. *(Isn't that weird?)* Okay …

ETHAN. I'm — gonna go write, okay? I gotta — get some of this down, okay?

MICHAEL. Of course. Are you…?

ETHAN. *(A little too sharply.)* I'm *fine*, Michael, okay? *(Ethan exits. Michael continues to the audience:)*

MICHAEL. *(Continued, to the audience.)* And so, for the next two weeks, Ethan vanished. Not literally, but he … went to that place where writers (me included) go sometimes to … get lost. That's how Joyce Carol Oates described it during our interview: "We get lost and then start stringing words together until we get back to where everyone else is — don't we?" she said, and I remember I kept meaning to share that with Ethan. I would join him, after work, in our living room, and I'd be writing, too — my novel — and I would remember that quote … but then his cell phone would ring, and it would be his agent (wanting to make sure Ethan was working on a new play; he wasn't), or his editor at DC Comics, or his father, or Mary Ellen from California, and he'd get up off and go into our bedroom for these secret conversations, and afterwards he would come back and — *(Ethan returns.)* — Who was that?

ETHAN. Oh, it was just … *(Ethan sits down, opposite Michael, immediately distracted.)*

MICHAEL. *(To audience.)* And this went on for two weeks, at which point Ethan sent Mary Ellen another batch of pages and waited for her phone call, which came the next day — *(Ethan's cell phone starts to ring and Ethan starts to get up.)* No, don't bother, I'll go. *(Michael exits and a spot comes up on Mary Ellen.)*

MARY ELLEN. So Barry and I read your new opening, and it's good. It's a lot *scarier* —

ETHAN. Great!

MARY ELLEN. But it needs something else —

ETHAN. Oh.

MARY ELLEN. It needs — the tragic boating accident.

ETHAN. The — ?

MARY ELLEN. The shipwreck that sets your entire story in motion? We need to *see* that shipwreck! *Visual medium*, Ethan, think *widescreen*.

ETHAN. So … out with the jellyfish, in with the shipwreck?

MARY ELLEN. Oh, no, no, we *love* the jellyfish. Barry especially, he hasn't set foot on our beach since he read those pages. No, Ethan, keep the jellyfish, *add* the shipwreck.

ETHAN. — Okay.

MARY ELLEN. And keep pushing forward. The rest of the story — it's really falling into place, I think.

ETHAN. Really? It's not too — I don't know — schematic?

MARY ELLEN. *(Gasping.)* There's no such thing, Ethan! There's too challenging and too original, but *never* too schematic! *(Ethan's cell phone beeps.)*

ETHAN. Oh, wait, Mary Ellen, it's my other line. Let me just get rid of —

MARY ELLEN. No, no, it's fine, go ahead, just keep sending me pages!

ETHAN. Oh — *(Mary Ellen hangs up.)* — kay. *(He clicks over.)* Hello? *(Spot on Tyler, in his office at DC Comics.)*

TYLER. *Bro, good news!*

ETHAN. Hi, Tyler.

TYLER. The Flash revealing his secret identity to Linda Parks? It's playing like *gangbusters!*

ETHAN. *(Incredulously.)* Really?

TYLER. Do you read these fan-sites? On the web? These online reviews?

ETHAN. No, for my sanity, I try not to —

TYLER. Good, you shouldn't, they're a bunch of serial-killers living in their mothers' basements, but — *but* — since your "Secret Revealed" issue, they've been *loving* you!

ETHAN. Are you joking?

TYLER. We're getting reorders — issues are flying off the shelves like *Superman*, bro.

ETHAN. Wow.

TYLER. Which means that now, more than ever, we gotta keep the book on schedule.

ETHAN. *(To audience.)* I hear you — *(Ethan's cell phone beeps.)* Oh — hey — Tyler, it's my other line —

TYLER. No problem — and great job on the latest issue, by the way. I love that you brought back the Pied Piper. *(Tyler hangs up as Ethan clicks over.)*

ETHAN. Hello? *(A spot comes up on Ethan's Dad.)*

ETHAN'S DAD. Ethan?

31

ETHAN. Dad — *hi* ...

ETHAN'S DAD. How are you? Busy, I imagine, since you haven't returned any of my phone calls —

ETHAN. Yeah, Dad — No, I *have* been busy, sorry — but I'm ...

ETHAN'S DAD. Good, busy's good ...

ETHAN. I — I know why you're calling, Dad — why you've *been* calling.

ETHAN'S DAD. Oh?

ETHAN. I think — shot in the dark — but: You haven't told Mom yet and you want to make sure *I'm* not gonna crack and tell her about your sordid affair first.

ETHAN'S DAD. Ethan ...

ETHAN. That's pretty much it, right?

ETHAN'S DAD. Don't — *(Mini-beat.)* — You don't have to be disrespectful —

ETHAN. *Me? I'm* being disrespectful? *(Beat.)* Uh, Dad, have you thought about Mom for one second? In all this time — all these months? Because, newsflash, Dad: Every day that you *don't* tell her, it's like you're *lying* to her —

ETHAN'S DAD. I *shouldn't* have dropped this into your lap, Ethan. It was unfair of me to expect you to — *(Beat.) That's* why I've been calling. To talk to you, to tell you —

ETHAN. — But I don't *want* to talk, Dad. I actually would love to *never* talk about this *ever* again. I would love for you to stop this thing with this woman —

ETHAN'S DAD. *(Getting angry himself.)* She has a name —

ETHAN. — Yeah, and it's so *nice* to be able to put a name to the person you currently hate most in the world!

ETHAN'S DAD. If you can't discuss this like an adult —

ETHAN. — and if you are going to continue this —

ETHAN'S DAD. — *relationship* —

ETHAN. — *affair. (Beat.)* If you're going to insist on doing this, then I am begging you to please not be a coward and tell Mom *now,* so that she can go to pieces and start getting over this betrayal.

ETHAN'S DAD. What made me think you would understand?

ETHAN. I truly have no idea! And understand *what,* P.S? That you *lied* — that you've *been* lying for I don't know how long?

ETHAN'S DAD. That I want to be happy. That I am finally allowing myself to be with someone who makes me happy and whom I make happy, as well. *(Beat.)* Because that is *not* the case with your mom and me, Eath, I'm sorry.

ETHAN. Me, too.

ETHAN'S DAD. And for the record, this is killing me. Knowing that my happiness is going to hurt your mother.

ETHAN. Why did you marry her, Dad? I mean, did you *ever* love her?

ETHAN'S DAD. If I could tell you why I made any of the decisions I've made over the last thirty years — *forty* years …

ETHAN. Okay, now this is — *(Mini-beat.)* — I mean, *really* absurd, Dad, you're being totally —

ETHAN'S DAD. What would you like me to say, Ethan? Tell me and I'll say it.

ETHAN. Dad … *(For a moment or two, it seems that Ethan might be relenting, but then:)* You know what, Dad, I actually don't think there's *anything*. *(Ethan shuts his cell phone, and the lights on Ethan's Dad go out. Michael enters, semi-distressed.)*

MICHAEL. *Ethan…? What's going on?*

ETHAN. Nothing. *(He puts on a hollow smile.)* Absolutely nothing, Michael.

MICHAEL. You were yelling, sweetie. I could hear you through the wall.

ETHAN. Michael, it's *fine*.

MICHAEL. Obviously it's not fine, Ethan, look at you, you're completely stressing out.

ETHAN. Yeah, I know, Michael, because I have — a *million* vague deadlines, in case you haven't been keeping track. Because I'm sinking all of my time and energy into a screenplay — which, by the way, is the first one I've ever written — and in the end it may all come to nothing. Because it's been *months* since I've even thought about starting a new play. Because my father is — *(Ethan stops himself.)*

MICHAEL. What? Tell me!

ETHAN. Tell you *what*? It's *nothing! (Beat.)* God. *(Beat.)* There's a lot on my plate — that's *all*. *(Beat.)* And, unfortunately, none of what I'm working on is a *novel*, which I can write whenever the spirit *moves* me. If I miss a deadline for *The Flash*, I can't just say: "Oops, sorry."

MICHAEL. I know.

ETHAN. Do you? Do you know that if I don't send my *Flash* script in on time, the guy who draws *The Flash* can't work, and if he can't work, he doesn't get paid, and — unlike me — he has an actual, real-life family to support?

MICHAEL. Yes, I know.

ETHAN. And do you know that breaking into movies is maybe the hardest thing *ever,* and that right now there's this tiny window I might just *barely* squeak through? That is *shrinking* every second?

MICHAEL. *(Biting back his anger.)* Yes, Ethan.

ETHAN. Then why, Michael, are you *harassing* me? Why are you, like, *breathing* down my neck, *demanding* to know what's wrong?

MICHAEL. *(Now* really *biting back his anger.)* You know what, Ethan, you can just go —

ETHAN. — Wait, Michael, I ... I didn't *really* say all those things, did I? Back then?

MICHAEL. Yeah, Eath, you did.

ETHAN. Just out of the blue like that? I just — exploded?

MICHAEL. You were keeping everything inside and you just —

ETHAN. — Like a landmine —

MICHAEL. — I just stepped on you, apparently. *(Short pause full of regret.)*

ETHAN. If I could go back in time on the Flash's cosmic tread-mill —

MICHAEL. Yeah, me too. *(With that, Michael exits and Ethan turns back to the audience.)*

ETHAN. *(To audience.)* I rewrote the opening the way Mary Ellen wanted me to and kept pushing forward. I hit page fifty, I hit page sixty. I sent the pages off to Mary Ellen, pulled an all-nighter to finish the latest issue of *The Flash,* which I did, I e-mailed it to Tyler, then slept eighteen hours straight. Page sixty-five — (I apologized to Michael a million different ways.) — Page seventy — (whenever my cell phone rang and I saw it was a Philly area-code, I didn't answer) — Page eighty — (Mary Ellen called back ...) *(Spot on Mary Ellen.)*

MARY ELLEN. Ethan, we're at Tommy's soccer game during a time out, but I had to call you: This new opening with the ship-wreck is — very, very real, very, very, harrowing.

ETHAN. Good, that's what I intended.

MARY ELLEN. But I was thinking — and Barry, too — that it's *still* not quite right.

ETHAN. Pardon?

MARY ELLEN. So we were wondering: What if you start with a nightmare? With the mother *jolting* awake from a nightmare?

ETHAN. A...?

MARY ELLEN. A *scary* one, Ethan. Something with monsters!

ETHAN. Uhm … But if I start with a nightmare, Mary Ellen …

MARY ELLEN. — Yes, tell me.

ETHAN. … What would it *mean?*

MARY ELLEN. Oh, Ethan, *no,* you're thinking too hard —

ETHAN. I am?

MARY ELLEN. You are. So lose the shipwreck, add a nightmare, and keep the jellyfish, of course, we still love those — and Ethan? *(He looks at her.)* You're doing a great job, keep pushing forward, and don't forget to tie up loose ends! *(Spot on Mary Ellen goes out and Ethan is alone again.)*

ETHAN. *(To audience.)* Which is what I did, all the way up to page … 105. *(POP! Michael enters with a gushing bottle of champagne and two glasses. Ethan turns to him confusedly.)* What's…?

MICHAEL. We're celebrating.

ETHAN. We are?

MICHAEL. You finished your screenplay …

ETHAN. You're late, sweetie, I finished it two weeks ago.

MICHAEL. I know, but since you sent it in: no insane phone calls from Mary Ellen —

ETHAN. Probably she hates the ending —

MICHAEL. — You've been sleeping semi-normal hours again —

ETHAN. Thank you, Tylenol PM.

MICHAEL. — I came up with a title for my novel —

ETHAN. — You did! What is it? —

MICHAEL. — We haven't fought, or come close to fighting, in days —

ETHAN. *(Instantly wary.)* — Yeah, I was wondering when and if we were ever gonna talk about that.

MICHAEL. Well, I wanted to wait for you to get over your hump.

ETHAN. Oh, no, that wasn't a hump, that was just — that's just how my life is now. *(Uh-oh. Which brings everything to a screeching halt. Definitely not the thing to say. Way to go, Ethan.)* That was a joke, by the way.

MICHAEL. I know, but …

ETHAN. Come on, Michael —

MICHAEL. … it's also *not* a joke, Ethan. *(Short pause.)*

ETHAN. Yikes, I am feeling *such* dread right now.

MICHAEL. This isn't right, Ethan. You *know* this isn't right.

ETHAN. No, I don't.

MICHAEL. Ethan …

ETHAN. What, Michael, I don't. *(Beat.)* I'm sorry, but I actually *do* think this is right. You, me, us, what we have — it's right. If it wasn't — if I didn't believe that — I wouldn't fight you about it, but I don't *not* think this isn't right. *(Beat.)* Wait, was that — ?

MICHAEL. There will *always* be a play —

ETHAN. — There isn't one right now —

MICHAEL. — or a screenplay, or another comic book — or another phone call — or another *series* of phone calls — that will take precedence.

ETHAN. Over what?

MICHAEL. Oh, come on, Ethan, I *will* say it if you make me.

ETHAN. But this has been — these last couple of months have been — an anomaly.

MICHAEL. You've been working on your screenplay for almost as long as we've been dating.

ETHAN. Yeah, but it's over — I'm done — no more screenplay, no more insane pressure coming from the other side of the country —

MICHAEL. Until Mary Ellen calls — *(At which point Ethan's cell phone starts to ring. Again Michael and Ethan just freeze. A beat, then:)*

ETHAN. I'm not gonna answer that.

MICHAEL. Just get it, it doesn't matter.

ETHAN. I'm serious, I'm not — *(He takes out the cell phone.)* — here, look. *(Almost triumphantly, Ethan turns off his cell phone, which cuts off in mid-ring.)* You were saying…?

MICHAEL. That's a very nice gesture, but it doesn't *change* anything.

ETHAN. I turned off my cell phone. From now on, I will *always* turn off my — *(At which point, the regular phone in the guys' living room starts to ring, shrilly.)* I'm not gonna get that. It could be Scott Rudin and I wouldn't get that. *(At an impasse, Ethan and Michael let the phone ring until their answering machine picks up:)*

ANSWERING MACHINE. Hi, there. This is Ethan … *(Michael's voice.)* And Michael … *(Back to Ethan.)* And neither one of us is here to take your call but please … *(Michael.)* Leave a message and your phone number … *(Ethan and Michael.)* And one or both of us will call you back as soon as possible.

MICHAEL. We should think about maybe changing that.

ETHAN. Michael — *(The answering machine beeps and a spot comes up on Ethan's Dad, leaving a message.)*

ETHAN'S DAD. Hello, Ethan and Michael, this message is for

Ethan … It's your dad, calling to say that … you're right, and …
I'm going to tell her … tonight.

MICHAEL. Tell who what?

ETHAN'S DAD. So please … call me when you get this, all right?
I'll … We'll be at home, I'm sure, and … I'd love to hear from you.
(Another beep and the spot on Ethan's Dad goes out.)

MICHAEL. Who is your dad gonna tell?

ETHAN. Nobody, Michael, it's just — family stuff. It's nothing
important.

MICHAEL. If it's a part of your life, I wanna know about it. If it's
something I can help you with —

ETHAN. Trust me — you can't.

MICHAEL. *No,* Ethan — *you* trust *me.* Let me in. *(And Michael
waits, and after a few moments, Ethan starts shaking his head.)*

ETHAN. Honestly, if there were something to tell you …

MICHAEL. You know what? You're an asshole, Ethan. Not — all
the time, but a lot of it.

ETHAN. Why? Because there are some things I want to keep pri-
vate? Things that, by the way, have nothing to do with you.
(Michael reacts.) What? They don't.

MICHAEL. You honestly don't get it, do you? What it means to be
in — *(The phone in the living room starts to ring again —)* God, I
should *rip* that fucking thing out of the wall!

ETHAN. What it means to be *what,* Michael?

MICHAEL. *In a relationship, Ethan!* In a real, living, breathing,
adult relationship! With another real, living adult person. Not with
a producer you've never met in Los Angeles, not with a comic book
character, not with the people who handle your career — I mean
with your *boyfriend! (The answering machine picks up again.)*

ANSWERING MACHINE. Hi, there. This is Ethan …
(Michael's voice.) And Michael … *(Back to Ethan.)* And neither one
of us is here to take your call but please … *(Michael.)* Leave a message and your phone number … *(Ethan and Michael.)* And one or
both of us will call you back as soon as possible. *(A spot light on
Mary Ellen, leaving a message.)*

MARY ELLEN. Ethan, it's Mary Ellen, I was going to wait until
I got home, but I'm stuck in traffic …

MICHAEL. Just answer it for God's sake — !

ETHAN. No, I don't care what she has to say, it can wait.

MARY ELLEN. Anyway, I got what you sent me, and Barry and

37

I read it, and we love it …

MICHAEL. Well, now we're *really* done.

ETHAN. No, we're not. I'm here, I'm not picking up —

MARY ELLEN. … It all really, really works …

ETHAN. I love you, Michael.

MARY ELLEN. … and Barry and I sent it out to a couple of the studios …

MICHAEL. This isn't something we can fix just like that, Ethan. With words.

ETHAN. Yeah, but did you hear me?

MARY ELLEN. … including Dreamworks …

ETHAN. I'm serious, I love you.

MARY ELLEN. … and Steven Spielberg wants to direct it, and Tom Hanks wants to play the dad, and Dreamworks wants to pay you seven hundred and fifty thousand dollars for it — *(Mini-beat.)* — so call me, kiddo, as soon as you can! *(The machine beeps again and the spot on Mary Ellen goes out. Neither Michael nor Ethan know what to say. Then:)*

MICHAEL. Ethan…?

ETHAN. That was … That's not …

MICHAEL. … Yeah, you should call her back right now. *(Quick blackout.)*

End of Act One

ACT TWO

The lights come up on Ethan and his dad, sitting side-by-side on chairs.

ETHAN. *(To audience.)* Ever since his first appearance in *Flash Comics #1*, the Flash has been able to do this really amazing thing. Move so fast he can be in two places at once. Or be in the same place as both Wally West *and* the Flash. *(Ethan considers this.)* I think that's why — growing-up — he was my favorite super-hero. *(Beat.)* Certainly, it's his super-power I envy most. The ability to be everywhere at once. To be wherever he's needed. To be *whatever* is needed at the moment. *(Ethan changes gears.)* The flight from New York to Los Angeles feels interminable.

ETHAN'S DAD. Are you going to eat your blue corn chips? Because if you *aren't* — *(Silently, Ethan hands his chips to his dad.)*

ETHAN. *(To audience.)* My dad isn't really here — on the plane.

ETHAN'S DAD. Is this my armrest or yours? Because we could divide it —

ETHAN. *(To audience.)* He's back in Philadelphia, doing — I'm sure — exactly what I'm doing.

ETHAN'S DAD. These seats are narrow, don't you think? And how's your seatbelt? Mine's —

ETHAN. *(To audience.)* Replaying our conversation — the conversation we had earlier this week — over and over, in his head.

ETHAN'S DAD. I told her, Ethan, I told your mother.

ETHAN. *(To audience.)* This is what's called "compression." "Streamlining." Which I can do because … I'm the writer.

ETHAN'S DAD. Last night, over dinner, I just decided and … started saying the words: "I don't love you anymore. I fell in love with someone else. I'm sorry. I'm sorry."

ETHAN. How did she — take it? Was she — heart-broken?

ETHAN'S DAD. She seemed … oddly relieved, mostly.

ETHAN. Mom did?

ETHAN'S DAD. I'm sorry if that disappoints you, Ethan. The —

the playwright in you. No big, dramatic blowout. No last-minute change of heart —

ETHAN. No — *Dad* — it just … surprises me, is all.

ETHAN'S DAD. She'd been feeling the same way I had for … years.

ETHAN. You said that, yeah.

ETHAN'S DAD. But to hear her admit it … After this … *sigh,* Ethan … This enormous release … *(He smiles grimly.)* It hurt me terribly to hear her say that she didn't love me — *(Mini-beat.)* — isn't that ridiculous?

ETHAN. Not at all …

ETHAN'S DAD. And afterwards — what happened after she sighed and told me she didn't love me —

ETHAN. What?

ETHAN'S DAD. I said: "So really, we're the same." And she said, "No, Gerald, *I* never would have done anything about my feelings. I never would've acted on them. I would've lived this way forever."

ETHAN. *Mom* said that?

ETHAN'S DAD. You should try calling her, Ethan. Your sister's with her at the house, but she'd love to hear from you, I'm sure.

ETHAN. I do — I will — I just … Wow. So then what happened?

ETHAN'S DAD. She said: "I'm assuming another woman's involved?"

ETHAN. Wow, this is so like a *telenovela.* And you said?

ETHAN'S DAD. "Yes," and she nodded — twice — and then she said: "I assume you're moving out now?"

ETHAN. Wow. And you said?

ETHAN'S DAD. "Yes," and she nodded — just once this time — and then we finished eating supper and watched the news.

ETHAN. Wow, that's totally … *(Beat.)* The important thing, though, is — you came clean with her, Dad.

ETHAN'S DAD. I certainly did.

ETHAN. And did Janice tell her husband?

ETHAN'S DAD. The same night I told your mother.

ETHAN. Well, that's … I mean, that's good, right? *(Beat.)* I mean, hard and awful, but now at least you guys can do … whatever you want to, right? Guilt-free?

ETHAN'S DAD. Not entirely. Guilt … sticks around, you'll learn, and Janice …

ETHAN. (Oh, God, what?)

ETHAN'S DAD. Janice started to — no, she *did* tell her husband — everything — but then he started crying, which started her crying, and then they started talking — about all their problems, their lives — and then ... *(Shakes his head.)* I'm not sure what, but Janice changed her mind.

ETHAN. What? Are you serious?

ETHAN'S DAD. She's not leaving her husband, and she can't see me anymore, she says.

ETHAN. *What? (Beat.)* And — and was *she* being serious?

ETHAN'S DAD. Utterly. *(He grimaces.)* So I went back to your mother and begged her to forgive me, to forget everything I'd said, but she ... Her heart tightened into this ... fist, and she socked me, she said: "Don't you understand, Gerald? You've *ruined* it. You said it aloud — you made *me* say it out loud — and now we can't *un*-say it."

ETHAN. Dad, I'm so — God, I'm sorry ...

ETHAN'S DAD. So I was thinking ... if it's all right with you and Michael ... I was thinking I'd come stay for a few days. I don't think I should be in Philadelphia right now ...

ETHAN. Dad ...

ETHAN'S DAD. Just for a few days —

ETHAN. No, Dad, of course you can — I mean, you're always welcome — it's just ... I'm going to Los Angeles. *(Beat.)* A — a work thing.

ETHAN'S DAD. That's where you're flying right now? On this plane?

ETHAN. Yeah. For some meetings about my screenplay ...

ETHAN'S DAD. And I'm not here?

ETHAN. No, Dad, you're in Philly, I think. Packing — (God, I'm so sorry) — but you're packing your suitcases and saying goodbye to mom and ... checking into a hotel.

ETHAN'S DAD. As fast as that, everything falls apart ...

ETHAN. You'll be okay, Dad. Mom, too, you'll both be —

ETHAN'S DAD. — Of course we will. *(Brave face.)* Call me when you get back, all right?

ETHAN. Absolutely. *(Ethan's Dad stands, starts to exit.)* Dad...?

ETHAN'S DAD. Hm?

ETHAN. ... Nothing. Not a thing. *(Ethan's Dad exits. Ethan turns to the audience. He's shaken, but he puts on as sunny a disposition as possible. To audience:)* Meanwhile! Back in the present — *(Becoming overwhelmed.)* I'm sorry, I just ... I got to L.A., I talked to my

41

mom, and it's just ... *(He shakes it off.)* — Anyway! In the home office of Barry and Mary Ellen Eustice! *(Mary Ellen enters, sits across from Ethan.)*

MARY ELLEN. Ethan — sweetheart — welcome to the place where dreams come true every day! How was your flight?

ETHAN. Fine, just —

MARY ELLEN. So. You're in Los Angeles!

ETHAN. Yeah.

MARY ELLEN. What do you think? Completely different from New York, right?

ETHAN. From the rest of the planet, actually.

MARY ELLEN. So, Ethan, Barry's in meetings all day and Tommy's at school, so it's just us, just us girls — and I'm wondering: Do you want the good news or the bad news first?

ETHAN. There's bad news?

MARY ELLEN. There's not-so-great news. *(Ethan is silent.)* So — to recap — there's good news and there's not-so-great news. Which would you like first?

ETHAN. I'm pretty emotionally raw, so maybe the good news?

MARY ELLEN. I'll give you the not-so-great news first, which is: The offer on your screenplay has been withdrawn.

ETHAN. *(To audience.)* Okay, if this were a movie? *(Beat.)* The camera would zoom in for a close-up on my face — on the look of horror/confusion on my face. Because this is real-life, though ... *(Turns to Mary Ellen, big smile.)* Whatever do you mean, Mary Ellen?

MARY ELLEN. The offer — if it ever really existed — is no longer on the table.

ETHAN. But what happened to Steven Spielberg?

MARY ELLEN. Best not to ask.

ETHAN. Tom Hanks?

MARY ELLEN. You don't want to go there.

ETHAN. I — I'm not sure I understand what's —

MARY ELLEN. — What's happening here happens all the time, so don't feel too bad about it and don't take it too personally, all right? Because it has *nothing* to do with the quality of your script, which is — high, *high* quality. *(Shrugs.)* It's just the way things go. Studio executives get hired, then get fired. Projects that had been given the green light disappear into a vault, never to be heard from again. The hottest script today is tomorrow's lunch-wrapper.

ETHAN. Is my script — ?

MARY ELLEN. *No.* No, not your script. Because remember: I have good news.

ETHAN. Better than: "Steven Spielberg and Tom Hanks want to do your movie"? *(Mary Ellen considers this.)*

MARY ELLEN. *Different* news. Because, anticipating these kinds of studio shenanigans, I took the liberty of slipping your screenplay to another director who read it and loves it and maybe wants to do it.

ETHAN. Maybe?

MARY ELLEN. Yes, well, he has some notes, of course. Some concerns.

ETHAN. Who — is this person?

MARY ELLEN. He's German, which is very exciting, his name's Thor, Thor Grunewald, he's very talented.

ETHAN. Would I know his work?

MARY ELLEN. Did you see *Stuart Little*?

ETHAN. No — *(Giving the devil his due.)* — but I heard it was okay.

MARY ELLEN. Yes, well, Thor was the second-unit director on *Stuart Little 2.*

ETHAN. Great, but has he actually directed anything for *real*?

MARY ELLEN. A short that was very well received at Sundance, a commercial for Nike that aired during the Super Bowl, and a music video for Green Day.

ETHAN. *(To audience.)* The pit in my stomach? Widening and deepening by the second. My hands? Clenched into fists. My fingernails? Digging into my palms. *(Beat.)* Nevertheless, I *somehow* manage to ask — *(Back to Mary Ellen.)* — what were his notes?

MARY ELLEN. Let me see if I can — *(Finds them on her desk.)* — all righty, here they are. Now do you want me sugar-coat them or just —

ETHAN. — Just give them to me straight-up.

MARY ELLEN. *(Looks down at the sheet, starts reading.)* "Needs more tension, needs more scares, needs stronger beginning, has too many characters, paced too much like a drama, the backstory is too complicated, too confusing, the dialogue is too real-sounding, the third-act needs to have a complication, can we make the mom's younger sister a detective or a sheriff?" — ooh, that's intriguing! — "Can either the mom or the dad have had an affair? — "

ETHAN. *(Interrupting.)* Okay, *what?*

MARY ELLEN. Our German *wunderkind* is wondering if the mother and/or the father in your screenplay can have had an affair in the past?

ETHAN. *Why?*

MARY ELLEN. To make their relationship more credible, more fraught with tension … To give the actors something to play …

ETHAN. No, I — I — I'm sorry, but no.

MARY ELLEN. No?

ETHAN. There is a *monster from the ocean* coming after their son — that is *plenty* for them to play. No, I *refuse* to give the mother and/or the father in my movie a sordid past — an affair on the recommendation of some *Nike* director —

MARY ELLEN. Ethan —

ETHAN. *(Overwrought.)* No, Mary Ellen, my parents are in a wonderful, loving, committed, healthy relationship. They are not fraught with — with — with *tension*. With — with — with *secrets*. With *lies*. With *deception*. With *betrayal*. They are *wonderful fucking people! (Short pause.)*

MARY ELLEN. You're overwrought.

ETHAN. No, really, I'm fine, that was —

MARY ELLEN. Your first time in Los Angeles, your first bitter taste of Hollywood, it's overwhelming —

ETHAN. No, no, it's fine —

MARY ELLEN. Take a break, get some sleep, get some sun. You don't want to meet with Thor —

ETHAN. But I *want* —

MARY ELLEN. — Let me make some calls, let me follow up with some people, let me see what bones I can rattle —

ETHAN. But I really do —

MARY ELLEN. *(Definitively.)* I will call you, Ethan.

ETHAN. — Okay. *(Mary Ellen stands, exits, and her office goes away. Ethan moves to another part of the stage and starts to undress. Takes off his shirt and pants — so that he's in a bathing suit, sitting by the pool. To audience:)* On my way back to the hotel — to sit by a pool — I started thinking about that dead kid from my play. The one I had brought back to life in my screenplay? I wondered if he wasn't haunting me now like … the ghosts in all those Asian horror movies? Their stringy hair like jellyfish tendrils? Was I experiencing a kind of … supernatural retribution? Because I had resurrected him when I should have left at the bottom of the ocean? *(Beat.)* I … reminded myself of all the good things in my life. That I chronicled the monthly adventures of the Fastest Man Alive. That any time I wanted to, I could go back to being a playwright. That maybe my family *was* falling apart, but I still had — *(Very quickly he pulls out his cell phone, dials. Spot on Michael, at his desk, answering.)*

MICHAEL'S VOICE. — This is Michael.

ETHAN. Hi …

MICHAEL. Hi, how's L.A.?

ETHAN. Oh, awful. It's sunny, it's hot, the air's terrible, everybody's skinny and shallow. How's New York?

MICHAEL. The same, except it's — *(Checks out his window.)* — it actually just started to snow.

ETHAN. Oh, I bet that's nice.

MICHAEL. Yeah, it's gonna put everybody in a *great* mood going home tonight.

ETHAN. I wish I was there.

MICHAEL. Why, is Tom Hanks being awful? (You didn't bring up *Philadelphia*, did you?)

ETHAN. No, no, the deal, the whole deal …

MICHAEL. What?

ETHAN. Oh, nothing, just the usual Hollywood bullshit …

MICHAEL. You didn't meet with Tom Hanks? He "sent somebody" instead?

ETHAN. No, no, it wasn't — totally like that …

MICHAEL. What, then?

ETHAN. I don't know, I just — I guess maybe I just miss you is all.

MICHAEL. Ethan …

ETHAN. What, is it not okay for me to miss you now?

MICHAEL. If that's what you're feeling …

ETHAN. It is; why, what are you — ?

MICHAEL. I think … I've been thinking I should maybe move out.

ETHAN. Hang on. Before I came out here, you told me you weren't going to make any rash —

MICHAEL. — This isn't. *(Beat.)* Look, nothing's final, nothing's been decided —

ETHAN. — except that you don't want to live together anymore!

MICHAEL. — Until we sort things out, no, maybe we shouldn't.

ETHAN. Michael. Renting another apartment in this market is *insane!*

MICHAEL. I'm not, I'd — probably, I'd stay with Greg.

ETHAN. *Greg, your ex-boyfriend?*

MICHAEL. Just until we figure out what we're — what you and

45

I — are doing, yes.

ETHAN. *Greg, your ex-boyfriend, who — P.S. — is still in love with you?*

MICHAEL. Oh, Ethan, he's a *friend*. He has a couch.

ETHAN. Are we breaking up, Michael?

MICHAEL. I don't know, Ethan. *(Beat.)* I know you want me to tell you that we're not, that this is just a rough patch, that everything's going to be all right, but I honestly ... Honestly, I don't know.

ETHAN. So, what then — this a break? Are we "Taking Some Time"?

MICHAEL. No, we're ... *I'm* in New York, you're in Los Angeles, we're waiting to figure things out until you get back — end of story.

ETHAN. I totally hate this.

MICHAEL. Me, too. Believe me.

ETHAN. I mean, do you even *miss* me?

MICHAEL. Of course I do.

ETHAN. Well — I mean — can I call you later?

MICHAEL. Of course you can.

ETHAN. Or — you know — *you* could call me ...

MICHAEL. I will — tonight — I promise.

ETHAN. Okay, well ... love you.

MICHAEL. Don't — *(Mini-beat.)* — don't get sunburned, okay? *(Michael hangs up and the spot on him goes out. At which point: Shirtless, wearing sunglasses, a towel around his shoulders, Hot L.A. Guy saunters on, approaches Ethan, starts stretching in a, let's say ... provocative way.)*

HOT L.A. GUY. 'S up?

ETHAN. Hi ...

HOT L.A. GUY. You're from New York, aren't you?

ETHAN. Excuse me?

HOT L.A. GUY. 'Cause you don't look like you're from L.A. —

ETHAN. Pasty arms, yeah ...

HOT L.A. GUY. — and, well, *everyone's* from New York.

ETHAN. ... Guilty.

HOT L.A. GUY. Yeah, I thought that. And you're a ... writer?

ETHAN. I am. *(Beat.)* And you're tan and blond and incredibly flexible, which means ... you're an actor?

HOT L.A. GUY. Trying to be. You a screenwriter?

ETHAN. Trying to be. Mostly I'm a playwright and I write comic books.

46

HOT L.A. GUY. No kidding, which ones?

ETHAN. Just one. *The Flash.* He's the one who —

HOT L.A. GUY. — runs really fast, yeah, I know, I'm actually going in for the movie version of *The Flash* next week.

ETHAN. Oh, cool. Orlando Bloom, he's …

HOT L.A. GUY. Any tips?

ETHAN. Tips…?

HOT L.A. GUY. Insights. For my audition. I'm reading for the Flash's best friend, the Pied Piper.

ETHAN. Insights …

HOT L.A. GUY. You being the writer of *The Flash* comic book and all …

ETHAN. Yeah, I might have some …

HOT L.A. GUY. … insights you could maybe …

ETHAN. … I could share them, yeah …

HOT L.A. GUY. I'd really — *really* — appreciate that…?

ETHAN. Ethan.

HOT L.A. GUY. Ethan — *(Beat.)* — hi. Is your room…?

ETHAN. Just right over …

HOT L.A. GUY. Excellent. *(The Hot L.A. Guy gets up and saunters off. Ethan turns to the audience.)*

ETHAN. I know. Believe me, I … *(Beat.)* In the history of bad ideas, this was *maybe* the worst one ever. *(Shakes his head.)* But it happened. And *after* it happened, I became overcome by this inexplicable need to — *confess,* to — *talk* to someone, *anyone.* But my friends are Michael's friends, and I didn't know anyone in L.A. except — *(Mary Ellen enters. As she crosses over to sit on the lounge chair across from Ethan:)*

MARY ELLEN. It's what Hollywood does best.

ETHAN. What's that?

MARY ELLEN. Corrupt.

ETHAN. They should put that on a billboard, as you're driving up into the Hollywood Hills … *(Grimaces.)* Thanks for coming, Mary Ellen. *(Gesturing.)* It's a nice hotel, don't you — ?

MARY ELLEN. — Do you know what Monroe Stahr, my first boss in the movie business, told me? He told me: "Everyone in Hollywood's unfaithful, Mary Ellen." (Anyone married, he meant.) "Because everyone in Hollywood has a first love — a *true* love — "

ETHAN. The movies?

MARY ELLEN. The movies.

ETHAN. I feel like I broke something, Mary Ellen.

MARY ELLEN. You did.

ETHAN. For good? For forever? *(Mary Ellen shrugs.)*

MARY ELLEN. Barry cheated on me once.

ETHAN. He did?

MARY ELLEN. With an actress. Famous, you'd know her. He told me, eventually. Years later.

ETHAN. What happened?

MARY ELLEN. It almost wrecked our marriage, Ethan — *and* ruined her career (and after we'd *made* her, the trollop). *(Beat.)* No, I forgave Barry, *that's* what happened. And slowly … we rebuilt.

ETHAN. What did — can I ask? — what did Barry say that made you forgive him?

MARY ELLEN. Say? Like dialogue you mean? *(Shakes her head.)* No, there wasn't anything Barry could say, I just … *(Looking right at Ethan.)* I forgave Barry because I knew he'd never forgive himself.

ETHAN. (Oh, God …) Even now?

MARY ELLEN. Even now, twenty years — twenty-*three* years — later. *(Beat.)* Oh, he forgets about what he did — sometimes for days at a stretch, even — but it's always there, Ethan. He can feel it. I can feel it.

ETHAN. But isn't that — ? That's so *sad*.

MARY ELLEN. That's living, my young screenwriter. Accumulating regret.

ETHAN. *(Asking "cosmically.")* God, what now?

MARY ELLEN. *(Laughing.)* You really are precious. *(Beat.)* You go back to New York, *that's* what's now. I send you back to New York, to cope with your father, and your boyfriend, and your comics, and the rest of your twenty-eight-year-old life. (My God, twenty-eight years old!)

ETHAN. But our meetings — ?

MARY ELLEN. Happened without you — as they should have, truthfully.

ETHAN. I went back to New York? Just like that?

MARY ELLEN. Flying first-class — only the best for my young F. Scott Fitzgerald!

ETHAN. And you'll call me? About the movie? Once you hear something?

MARY ELLEN. *Anything.* The second I hear anything, I'll call you — or Barry maybe, but probably it'll be me.

ETHAN. Thank you, Mary Ellen.

MARY ELLEN. A word of advice, Ethan —

ETHAN. "?"

MARY ELLEN. — Don't tell your beau what you did with that actron.

ETHAN. But Barry —

MARY ELLEN. Different circumstances, chum — and honesty's an over-rated virtue. *(She smiles — to encourage him.)* It's your mistake. *You* live with what you've done.

ETHAN. I — *(Nods.)* — okay.

MARY ELLEN. And then, after a few years, a few movies ... absolve yourself, okay?

ETHAN. Years?

MARY ELLEN. Hang in there, kiddo. *(And with that, Mary Ellen turns and exits.)*

ETHAN. *(To audience, to himself.)* I fly back to New York. (Don't tell Michael I cheated on him.) I take a cab from JFK into Manhattan. (Don't tell Michael I cheated on him.) On the way, I call Michael; he's at home. (No matter what, don't tell him I cheated on him.) I take the elevator up to the twelfth floor. (Don't tell Michael I cheated on him.) I walk down the long, black-and-white tiled hallway to my apartment's front door. (Don't tell Michael.) I put the key in the lock. (Please, God, let me not tell Michael.) I swing the door open, Michael is there (don't tell him), I set down my suitcase (don't you dare!), and he says: *(Michael enters like a beam of sunshine!)*

MICHAEL. *(Arms wide open.)* Home comes the conquering hero! Tell me everything!

ETHAN. Michael,Icheatedonyouwiththisguybythepoolwhowas blondandtanandtotallyvapidandI'msoincrediblysorrywillyoupleasef orgivemeI'lldoanything? *(Short pause.)*

MICHAEL. You ...

ETHAN. I ... I wasn't *supposed* to tell you —

MICHAEL. Ethan ...

ETHAN. — But I didn't want there to be this — this — this *lie* — this *thing* — between us.

MICHAEL. While we're in the middle of all this — all these *problems* — ?

ETHAN. *Challenges,* sweetie, *opportunities* — but I know. And believe me it was *awful.* I refuse to be a cliché and say it meant

49

nothing, but it honestly didn't. It was just this stupid, sordid, *meaningless* thing that — well, that I don't think either of us enjoyed. (I know *I* didn't …)

MICHAEL. Who, Ethan?

ETHAN. An actor — unspeakable, I know — I can't even remember his name —

MICHAEL. Oh, so this was *classy. (Beat.)* And — uhm — was this the first time you were — ?

ETHAN. *Michael — (Beat.)* — of *course.* How can you even ask that?

MICHAEL. Are you *joking?*

ETHAN. I have *never* been unfaithful to you —

MICHAEL. — Before this actor?

ETHAN. — I — *(Mini-beat.)* — admittedly, I'm on shaky ground here, but yes. Never.

MICHAEL. You … Oh, Ethan, you decided everything for us, you know. It's decided now.

ETHAN. Don't, Michael. Don't say that.

MICHAEL. I was actually thinking we could — that we *could* keep at it. Start over again once this insanity with your screenplay was over.

ETHAN. We can. I had the same thought.

MICHAEL. Before, after, or *while* you were fucking around with this guy?

ETHAN. Michael — *(Helpless.)* — weren't we Taking Some Time?

MICHAEL. *(Angry.)* Oh, that's really —

ETHAN. *(Also angry.)* Oh, well, excuse me for being confused, because didn't you tell me you wanted to move out?

MICHAEL. Which only meant that we needed a clean break to start over.

ETHAN. Fine, then — we'll wipe the slate clean, we'll start over!

MICHAEL. I don't think so.

ETHAN. Jesus, it was a mistake!

MICHAEL. Do you remember, Ethan, when we first met — at Java Boy — do you remember what I said to you?

ETHAN. Yes. You said —

MICHAEL. — "Hi, Tim?" *(Beat.)* Because I *thought* you were someone else because I was *there* to meet someone else. A friend of mine was fixing me up with someone named … Tim Miller. *(Beat.)* But I got it wrong, we were supposed to meet at Java *House,* not at

Java *Boy*. So when I realized you weren't Tim Miller, and I didn't see Tim Miller anywhere, I assumed I'd been stood up, so I asked if I could sit with you. But then, that night, my friend called me and explained that Tim Miller had been at Java House, that it had all been a misunderstanding, and that he was a wonderful guy and that I had to try to meet up with him again.

ETHAN. Tim Miller?

MICHAEL. *A medical student — The Holy Grail!* But I didn't because — I said to my friend — like an asshole I said: "I met this guy, and he's really cute, and he's really funny, and he's really smart, and I think we're going to try it." *(Beat.)* And *she* said, "Are you sure? Because Tim Miller's really amazing." And I said, "I'm sure," and now — I don't know how many months later — there's *nothing* to say.

ETHAN. I love you, Michael, and everything will fall apart if you leave — I could have said *that* to you. *(Short pause.)* I also could've said: "There is no money, there is no movie, there is just this fear that if it doesn't happen right now, *nothing* will ever happen with my career, and that without my career — if I'm not successful — how could someone as wonderful as you love me?" *(Beat.)* I could've, but …

MICHAEL. Ethan …

ETHAN. Part of me thinks I did what I did to give you a reason to leave me, Michael. Because if I hadn't pushed you away and you'd *still* left, what would that have meant? That I don't *deserve* to be with anyone?

MICHAEL. Ethan, everyone —

ETHAN. Or what if I *had* let you in completely and you decided I wasn't enough? Or you saw — or discovered — some ugly part of me — *then* what would I have had?

MICHAEL. Ethan, you should have said these — *those* — things to me that night …

ETHAN. Yeah, and also that my mom and dad were splitting up, P.S. *(Beat.)* That in the midst of all that screenplay madness, after thirty-three years, their entire lives — everything they knew — it was all falling apart.

MICHAEL. Your mom and dad were — back then — ?

ETHAN. Yeah, and if I had shared you with them, or told you about their divorce, that would've meant you were an important part of my life, which would've meant that I wasn't enough on my own.

MICHAEL. That doesn't even make —

ETHAN. I can do this one thing, Michael — write — but what happens if in a year — or in a month — what happens if I sit down to write and there's nothing left because I've given it all to you?

MICHAEL. Ethan, is this — *that's* what you were thinking? Seriously?

ETHAN. Yes. Not consciously, but yes. All year long, the night we broke up for good —

MICHAEL. Why didn't you tell me any of that? That — that last time in our apartment?

ETHAN. Michael … you don't spend twenty-eight years of your life *not* telling people things and then start telling them just like that.

MICHAEL. If you had …

ETHAN. Would you have stayed?

MICHAEL. No. *(Beat.)* But I wouldn't have been so angry.

ETHAN. Yeah … *(Short pause. Then:)*

MICHAEL. Well, I guess I …

ETHAN. — Don't go, Michael. *(Short pause.)* Forgive me — give me another chance.

MICHAEL. Ethan …

ETHAN. *I* would forgive *you.*

MICHAEL. I've tried, Ethan, I have, but …

ETHAN. I *hate* this part of the story. *(Michael feels something happening, reacts.)*

MICHAEL. God, this is awful. This is — *(Shakes his head, then to Ethan.)* — I'm going, I can't —

ETHAN. — All right, just —

MICHAEL. — Goodbye, Ethan. *(Michael goes, leaving Ethan alone.)*

ETHAN. Goodbye, Michael. *(Takes the fact that he and Michael are over.)* Oh, wow. Oh … my … *(Ethan's cell phone starts to ring. Taking deep breaths, Ethan answers it.)* Hello? *(Quick spot on Mary Ellen.)*

MARY ELLEN. You told him, didn't you?

ETHAN. I did.

MARY ELLEN. (You're such a writer.) And?

ETHAN. And … it's over.

MARY ELLEN. Oh, no, Ethan, nothing's ever over.

ETHAN. This is.

MARY ELLEN. Just until the director's cut of your relationship comes out on DVD with deleted scenes and an alternate ending. Just until the *remake* of it comes out — until its *sequel* —

ETHAN. Mary Ellen, I know you're trying to cheer me up —

MARY ELLEN. Three different studios want to make a deal with us — *(Short pause.)* — does *that* cheer you up? *(Ethan checks his heart.)*

ETHAN. Nope, I'm still depressed. I'm still —

MARY ELLEN. Well, Focus Features wants to make a deal with us, Beacon Pictures wants to make a deal with us, and HBO wants to make a deal with us. *(No response from Ethan, so she continues.)* Focus is offering us the most money, but they're notorious for buying scripts and then letting them languish.

ETHAN. *(Half to himself.)* Michael didn't ask for *anything* ...

MARY ELLEN. What? *(Ethan just shakes his head, sadly and slowly.)* Fine, but I hope you're hearing me, because you're going to have to make a decision very, very quickly. *(No reaction; she continues:)* Beacon's talking about less money, which is fine, but I'm a *smidge* concerned because they've never made this kind of movie before.

ETHAN. If I had given him a little bit more attention ...

MARY ELLEN. How about giving *me* some attention? Your break-up was *weeks* ago — *(To audience.)* literally; I'm hitting the fast-forward button on this part of story — *(Back to Ethan.)* HBO's offering us the least amount of money, but they're saying they can fast-track it into production by ... the end of the year, they say.

ETHAN. ... Fine.

MARY ELLEN. I'm sorry? Did you just — ?

ETHAN. Sell it to HBO.

MARY ELLEN. Are you sure? Because you can take a day or two if you want to —

ETHAN. No, HBO was — after the Food Network — Michael's favorite cable channel ...

MARY ELLEN. Understood, but something I want you to think about: It's *substantially* less money —

ETHAN. How much less?

MARY ELLEN. Maybe fifty, sixty thousand dollars total.

ETHAN. That's — enough.

MARY ELLEN. That's *peanuts,* Ethan, considering all the work we've done, but — *but* — they have a good director who's ready to move on it, whom of course you'll meet —

ETHAN. Not Thor?

MARY ELLEN. I swear to you: not Thor.

ETHAN. And you think it'll actually get made?

MARY ELLEN. My Magic 8 Ball says: "Most probably."

ETHAN. And once it's sold, I may have to do a rewrite —

MARY ELLEN. — or two, for which you'll get paid handsomely —

ETHAN. — but basically I can go back to — to writing just my comic books, maybe a play —

MARY ELLEN. — short stories, your *journal,* your blog, whatever — yes. *(Mini-beat.)* Until the next movie.

ETHAN. Sell it to HBO, Mary Ellen.

MARY ELLEN. I think it's the way to go.

ETHAN. Great.

MARY ELLEN. Ethan … *(Her heart goes out to him.)* I know it probably doesn't *feel* this way right now, but trust me: This is the start of something. Something *good.*

ETHAN. No, I know …

MARY ELLEN. All righty, then — I'll make the HBO thing happen.

ETHAN. You will?

MARY ELLEN. *(To audience.)* I did — contracts are in the mail.

ETHAN. *(To audience.)* I signed them. My friends took me to Chevy's to celebrate. All through dinner, I kept thinking: "Michael should be here."

MARY ELLEN. Give it time, Ethan. Time, the Great Destroyer, is also the Great Healer. *(Beat.)* Keep your phone on; I'll call with updates. *(So Ethan is once again alone on stage.)*

ETHAN. *(To audience.)* Which is what Mary Ellen does — did. Held my hand through pre-production, casting, rewrites, etc. etc. It was like … the weirdest part-time job in the world. *(Beat.)* I started keeping track of time by my movie's production schedule. I spent my days writing and doing rewrites, fighting the urge to call Michael every five seconds. At night, I wandered around our stupid apartment, like an extra from *Night of the Living* — *(Ethan's Dad enters with a suitcase. Lets it drop as he announces:)*

ETHAN'S DAD. It's *spacious,* Eath. I didn't think people like you could afford apartments this size in New York.

ETHAN. People like?

ETHAN'S DAD. Artists, bohemians …

ETHAN. Dad, I write *The Flash* for DC Comics, which is owned by Time Warner, which is owned by AOL, which is owned by Satan. Who pays exceedingly well.

ETHAN'S DAD. But you can actually *breathe* here. When you said I could stay with you until I find my own apartment —

ETHAN. *(To audience.)* This part of the story is about how my father, the most unlikely of super-heroes, saves my life.

ETHAN'S DAD. How long has it been now? Since you and Michael stopped — ?

ETHAN. — Since we broke up and Michael moved out? Three months, I think. *(Calculates.)* Almost three and a half.

ETHAN'S DAD. And how long were you together?

ETHAN. Almost a year. (You know this, Dad.)

ETHAN'S DAD. Living here in this apartment?

ETHAN. For most of that time, yeah.

ETHAN'S DAD. Do you think, maybe — *(Proceeding with caution.)* — I'm not saying you should, but have you thought about moving?

ETHAN. Not really. *(Beat.)* Plus, if I'm gonna do this — be a writer, I mean — if this is for the rest of my life, maybe I should make that extra room … a writing room. In earnest. Not just say that it is, but really make it … an office or whatever. Which I could write off on my taxes and … *(But Ethan's Dad is just staring at his son.)* Dad…?

ETHAN'S DAD. What you set out to do — be a writer? Carve out this kind of life? You've done it, son. You've really done it. *(Short pause, then:)*

ETHAN. I've made such a mess of things.

ETHAN'S DAD. … Michael?

ETHAN. I was really unfair to him. I really … took him for granted.

ETHAN'S DAD. Have you tried — ?

ETHAN. — Everything. It's … pretty over.

ETHAN'S DAD. For now it is. Maybe, in awhile, in a few months, in a year, you'll come together again.

ETHAN. I don't think so … *(Ethan almost starts crying — but doesn't.)*

ETHAN'S DAD. Ethan …

ETHAN. It just — really, really feels awful. I really, really hurt him, Dad.

ETHAN'S DAD. I know …

ETHAN. How do I make this go away? This feeling? How do I — *(Change of thought.)* — How did *you*, after Janice dumped you?

ETHAN'S DAD. I didn't — I haven't — yet.

ETHAN. Really? You seem fine.

ETHAN'S DAD. At a certain point, I think you just … decide how you're going to be. *(By way of example.)* "I'm okay with this." "I'm starting to get better." "I'm happy today." *(Turns to Ethan.)* You decide it, and then … eventually … it becomes true.

ETHAN. But until that happens…?

ETHAN'S DAD. You're a writer — *revise* yourself. (Think about it in those terms.) And the next time someone wonderful comes along —

ETHAN. I want Michael.

ETHAN'S DAD. — Michael, or someone else just as wonderful … you'll be ready to meet him. You won't make the same mistakes —

ETHAN. Never again —

ETHAN'S DAD. Look: Be sad about Michael, be regretful, mope if want to, if you need to, but don't *despair,* for God's sake. You hurt someone, now *you're* hurting. It's the way of the world …

ETHAN. It's still fucking shitty.

ETHAN'S DAD. Can I ask you something?

ETHAN. Sure.

ETHAN'S DAD. Since when has it been all right for you to swear in front of me?

ETHAN. *(To audience.)* You see? How he drags light and life back into my apartment, into my days?

ETHAN'S DAD. *(To audience.)* I encouraged Ethan, as much as possible, as gently as possible, to … you know … go out and date.

ETHAN. *(To audience.)* Gently? He posted listings on match.com, on nerve.com, on gay.com — he changed my Friendster profile to "single," he gave me *money* to go out on dates —

ETHAN'S DAD. It's important that both of us "put ourselves" out there, that we don't just work — *(Pointing offstage.)* It's okay if I take your bedroom? *(Ethan's Dad exits, pulling his suitcase off with him.)*

ETHAN. *(To audience.)* Though I did do a fair amount of work, too, in the months immediately following Michael and my — *(At which point, Tyler enters, clutching another sheaf of papers. We're in his office again.)*

TYLER. Bro, this issue …

ETHAN. You hate it, Tyler. You think it's self-indulgent.

TYLER. I think it's *harsh.* Does Linda *have* to dump Wally?

ETHAN. Tyler — *(Deep sigh.)* — yes.

TYLER. Because — and let me make sure I got this right — because she couldn't handle him being the Flash?

ETHAN. That right. She doesn't want to be a — I guess the term is "super-hero widow."

TYLER. Yeah, but getting dumped is so unheroic, bro

ETHAN. Bad things happen sometimes, Tyler. Even to …

TYLER. … super-heroes, I know, but couldn't she have embraced it?

ETHAN. Embraced...?

TYLER. Couldn't Linda have said: "I'm not crazy about you being the Flash, Wally, I'm not crazy about all the baggage that entails, the long hours, the risk, but I love you, and even though this is going to be hard, and it's going to require sacrifice, I accept every part of you and we're going to make this work." Couldn't *that* have been her reaction?

ETHAN. You guys *started* this, Tyler. You guys *wanted* Wally's character to deepen, to make him more of a "real" person ...

TYLER. Yeah, but this is *cold* ...

ETHAN. It'll open doors, Tyler, not — not close them. *(Tyler considers it for a few moments.)*

TYLER. Okay, let me see if I can —

ETHAN. — Yeah, see if you can push that through, okay? *(Tyler looks at Ethan, narrows his eyes. Ethan shakes his head, waves it off.)* I'd really appreciate that, Tyler.

TYLER. 'S what I'm here for, bro. *(Tyler exits; Ethan's Dad reenters, holding/reading a comic book.)*

ETHAN'S DAD. Son, don't you think Michael will read this issue and ... get the wrong idea?

ETHAN. Michael didn't read my comics while we were together, dad, I seriously doubt he's reading them now.

ETHAN'S DAD. How is Michael, anyway? Have you ... talked to him?

ETHAN. No, but he's ... His novel's getting — got — published.

ETHAN'S DAD. It did? That fast?

ETHAN. Well, I'm compressing again, but ... yeah, it happened pretty fast.

ETHAN'S DAD. While your movie was shooting on location in Newfoundland, don't forget.

ETHAN. Dad —

ETHAN'S DAD. Let me brag, Ethan. As your father, it is my God-given right to —

ETHAN. You do realize, Dad, that by this point you've moved out already? Moved to your — your "bachelor pad" on West End Avenue?

ETHAN'S DAD. I'm only saying —

ETHAN. *(To audience.)* — The point is, I *almost* e-mailed Michael to congratulate him, but then I actually read his novel, which was ... *(Ethan's Dad is now reading a copy of* The Lonely Boy in the Attic.*)*

ETHAN'S DAD. You know, this is quite good ... *(Ethan glares at his dad, turns back to the audience.)*

ETHAN. *(To audience.)* Michael did a reading at the Borders in the Time Warner Center that I, you know, crashed.

ETHAN'S DAD. Ethan ...

ETHAN. *(To audience.)* Don't worry, Dad, I sat in the back and wore sunglasses and snuck out before it was over.

ETHAN'S DAD. He didn't see you? You're sure?

ETHAN. No way, I'm getting very good at all these covert —

ETHAN'S DAD. Ethan —

ETHAN. — operations — what?

ETHAN'S DAD. You have to stop this, you know.

ETHAN. Stop...?

ETHAN'S DAD. And I've been thinking: You need to write a play.

ETHAN. A play? When my last play —

ETHAN'S DAD. — I know, never got produced. But honestly, son, it was a downer. And aren't you just starting out? Don't these things take time?

ETHAN. I guess ...

ETHAN'S DAD. Comic books are wonderful, this movie —

ETHAN. *(To audience.)* — Which is screening here in New York, at HBO. You have to come!

ETHAN'S DAD. — All those things are wonderful, but I really think you need to challenge yourself creatively, emotionally, open yourself up a bit, and —

ETHAN. — write a play?

ETHAN'S DAD. I think it's time. Besides, isn't it true that when playwrights aren't writing plays they're unhappy? Generally?

ETHAN. I think ... Edward Albee said that, yeah.

ETHAN'S DAD. I don't know about Edward Albee, but remember what *you* said to me when you told me you were going to grad school to study playwriting?

ETHAN. (Oh, God ...)

ETHAN'S DAD. You said (and this is a direct quote, I believe): "It's what makes me happiest and most fulfilled."

ETHAN. Really? That's very ... self-aware of me.

ETHAN'S DAD. "Writing plays is when I feel most confident and secure and human."

ETHAN. *(To himself.)* I used those words?

ETHAN'S DAD. "I'm more *open* when I'm writing a play, I sleep better when I'm writing a play, I play better with others when I'm writing a play, I — "

ETHAN. Okay —

ETHAN'S DAD. — So …

ETHAN. *(To audience.)* … I started writing a play. And pretty soon, I was done with Act One, and it was time for my screening. *(Beat.)* HBO said I could invite a few people, so … I did. *(Beat.)* My dad and mom —

ETHAN'S DAD. — I can tell them. *(To audience.)* Since our divorce, Ethan's mom and I have become …

ETHAN. I think the word is "friends," Dad. You and Mom are —

ETHAN'S DAD. *(To audience.)* — That's right, we're friends now.

ETHAN. *(To audience.)* It's true. You don't know this because you never got to see them together (my mom's already inside, saving seats), but there's an *ease* about them now. It's like for thirty years of their lives, they'd been carrying enormous bags of sand on their shoulders, and now …

ETHAN'S DAD. *(To audience.)* … Now we're *not.*

ETHAN. *(To audience.)* It makes me happy. *(Thinks about it.)* Happier.

ETHAN'S DAD. Ethan, do you know where I can buy popcorn?

ETHAN. Nowhere, dad, it's a *screening* in a *screening* room.

ETHAN'S DAD. *(Shaking his head in "cosmic" outrage.)* A movie without popcorn?

ETHAN. I'll — see you inside, Dad. *(Ethan's Dad moves to the back of the stage, sits down on a chair, facing downstage, where he'll be for the rest of the play. To audience:)* I invited Tyler, who showed up with — *(Tyler enters, makes a beeline for Ethan.)*

TYLER. I got news, bro. Big *effing* news.

ETHAN. Yes, Tyler?

TYLER. Frank Casey, the guy who's directing the *Flash* movie? He's been reading our comic book, and *he* thinks you've got the Flash's voice *nailed,* bro. He thinks it's *authentic.*

ETHAN. It's *my* voice, Tyler —

TYLER. — *Exactly* what I told him, bro, which is why he wanted me to ask you to ask your agent to give Warner Brothers a call because he —

ETHAN. — Frank Casey —

TYLER. — wants to meet with you to talk about possibly doing a polish on the screenplay.

ETHAN. On the *Flash* screenplay?

TYLER. Exactamundo.

ETHAN. Well — I mean — of *course* I'll do it. I mean, you don't *not* answer a call from Warner Brothers when it comes.

TYLER. I'm right there with you, bro.

ETHAN. Hey, Frank Casey hasn't cast it yet, has he? The movie?

TYLER. Not according to the serial killers living in their parent's basements, no.

ETHAN. Good, good … *(Turns back to Tyler.)* Yeah — no — that'll give me a chance to make sure he doesn't hire a certain sexually-ambiguous, social-climbing, vapid, shallow, blond actor I know to play the Pied Piper.

TYLER. Uh … *(Mary Ellen enters, waves to Ethan.)*

MARY ELLEN. Ethan!

TYLER. See you inside, bro — and congrats! *(Tyler moves to the chairs at the back of the stage. Takes a seat next to Ethan's Dad as Mary Ellen reaches Ethan.)*

MARY ELLEN. My God, how do you people *live* in this city?

ETHAN. It's not *that* bad …

MARY ELLEN. My God, the *filth,* the human degradation, the *cold* —

ETHAN. Hey, where's Barry? I mean, does he even exist, Mary Ellen?

MARY ELLEN. He's trying to find a parking spot —

ETHAN. You *drove?*

MARY ELLEN. We rented a car at the airport.

ETHAN. You rented a car in *New York?*

MARY ELLEN. Don't ask me, ask Barry — but Ethan!

ETHAN. What — what?

MARY ELLEN. You wrote a movie and I produced it and it got made and we're about to see it!

ETHAN. Yeah…?

MARY ELLEN. Ethan, that *never — ever —* happens!

ETHAN. I know.

MARY ELLEN. So be happy!

ETHAN. I am. *(Mary Ellen looks at Ethan.)*

MARY ELLEN. You're getting there.

ETHAN. I'm trying to …

MARY ELLEN. Well, guess what, while you're trying. Touchstone called.

ETHAN. Touchstone Pictures?

MARY ELLEN. Somehow they got a copy of your screenplay — hmm, I wonder how that happened — and they want to know if we're interested in developing a property they own.

ETHAN. Oh-kay …

MARY ELLEN. A remake of an old horror movie — yeah, I thought that might perk you up — a French one called *Eyes Without a Face*, do you know it? I think Criterion put out the DVD? *(At that moment, Michael walks on, carrying a wrapped bottle of champagne. Ethan sees him from across the stage.)*

ETHAN. Yeah, I saw it, believe it or not, about … a year and a half ago.

MARY ELLEN. Well, we should talk about whether or not we want to — *(Mary Ellen sees who Ethan is looking at, turns back to him. Gasping:)* — That's him, isn't it?

ETHAN. — Yeah —

MARY ELLEN. — Oooh, he's *cute* —

ETHAN. — *What?*

MARY ELLEN. — No, no, you're cuter, you're cuter — !

ETHAN. — Mary Ellen —

MARY ELLEN. — I know, why don't I go in and find a — ?

ETHAN. — Yeah, I think my mom's saving one for you up front.

MARY ELLEN. Up front?

ETHAN. *Mary Ellen —*

MARY ELLEN. I'm gone! *(Mary Ellen heads to the back of the stage, takes her seat. Ethan and Michael are alone on stage, eyeing each other warily — but, let's say it, warmly.)*

MICHAEL. Was that…?

ETHAN. Yeah, that was Mary Ellen, can you believe it?

MICHAEL. I thought she'd be …

ETHAN. Older?

MICHAEL. Foaming at the mouth, I was going to say.

ETHAN. Oh, no, she's not that bad. She's actually really … *(Awkward pause.)*

MICHAEL. So: your big movie.

ETHAN. Yes, well, since I couldn't get it produced as a play … *(Beat.)* Small movie, more like it. *HBO* movie …

MICHAEL. I *love* HBO. After the Food Network —

ETHAN. — It's your favorite channel, I know.

MICHAEL. I was surprised to get your invitation.

61

ETHAN. Well — I mean — you *were* there when this whole thing started …

MICHAEL. Yes, but after you came to my reading and snuck-out without saying "hi" or anything …

ETHAN. You — uhm — noticed that?

MICHAEL. … And with everything that's going on between Wally West and his girlfriend …

ETHAN. Wait, you're reading my comic book?

MICHAEL. … I have to say, I was a little worried, Ethan. I even almost called you. *(Beat.)* But looking at you now, you seem —

ETHAN. — Oh, yeah, I'm —

MICHAEL. — I'm glad.

ETHAN. And *you* seem — You look —

MICHAEL. — I'm great, I'm good. The book —

ETHAN. — Which I read and *loved,* by the way.

MICHAEL. Oh good, I was wondering.

ETHAN. I'm — glad you came, Michael, and — I'm sorry.

MICHAEL. For what?

ETHAN. For … not being ready to be in a relationship with you.

MICHAEL. It's all right, I … *(Beat.)* I understand — I think — a little bit. With the book — my book — and it just got optioned — I —

ETHAN. Wow, that's —

MICHAEL. — No, it's great, but it's made me understand, a bit, what you must have … *(Beat.)* Being pulled in so many … *(Beat.)* Juggling so much, it can be — it can *get* — overwhelming …

ETHAN. It can, yeah, but that's not really an excuse for what —

MICHAEL. — No, I know, but still … *(Beat.)* Are you seeing anyone?

ETHAN. Me? No one seriously, just … *(Shakes his head.)* No one seriously.

MICHAEL. Me, neither … *(Awkward pause.)*

ETHAN. Well, God, this is awkward *(Awkward pausing …)*

MICHAEL. Are you…? You working on anything new?

ETHAN. I … am, actually, yeah. A new play, believe it or not. *(Beat.)* Finally. After almost two years.

MICHAEL. What's it about?

ETHAN. Oh … it's this weird kind of … hard to describe comedy-slash-"relationship" play-slash — *(Beat.)* It's about us, Michael. It's about what happened to us. *(Beat.)* I'm the narrator in it. The "me character" is the narrator in it.

MICHAEL. Oh.

ETHAN. Well, I mean, the "me character" *is* a writer, so at least it makes dramaturgical sense.

MICHAEL. But I'm — my character — he's a writer, too, isn't he? *(Short pause. Ethan considers this.)*

ETHAN. Okay, well, maybe you can narrate a little bit of it.

MICHAEL. Okay, well, mostly I'm just giving you a hard time.

ETHAN. I know, I deserve — *(Michael suddenly, and quite wonderfully, hugs Ethan.)*

MICHAEL. — It's really good to see you, Ethan. *(The hug ends.)*

ETHAN. We should go in, it's gonna start …

MICHAEL. Yeah, and I'll … I'll see you afterwards?

ETHAN. Yeah, there's a reception, which is all about making me feel uncomfortable, I think, so …

MICHAEL. Congratulations, Ethan.

ETHAN. Thank you. *(Michael moves to the back of the stage, takes his seat. Ethan is unsure of what to say or do …)*

ETHAN. *(To audience.)* So…? Now…?

MARY ELLEN. Tie up loose ends, Ethan.

ETHAN. *(To audience.)* Right, loose ends …

TYLER. *(To audience, from the back of the stage.)* Tyler and Ethan Keene work together on *The Flash* for … almost four years. After they put their last issue to bed, Tyler takes Ethan out for a drink. "I feel like I'm losing one of my best friends," Ethan tells Tyler. "The Flash, bro?" "No, Tyler" Ethan says, "I'm talking about you."

MARY ELLEN. *(To audience, from the back of the stage.)* Mary Ellen and her husband continue doing what they've been doing for most of their lives: They make movies. Some good, some bad, some — a couple — scrape greatness. They never get an Oscar, though, their secret dream — (though they're nominated) — but somehow … that's the right ending for them.

ETHAN'S DAD. *(To audience, from the back of the stage.)* Ethan's dad and Janice *don't* come together again. They, in fact, never speak again. *(Beat.)* Ethan's dad and his mom don't come together again, either, but they remain friends for the rest of their lives. They even — believe it or not — attend each other's respective second weddings. (It's a *long* story …)

MICHAEL. *(To audience, from the back of the stage.)* Michael Sullivan writes several more books. After his second collection of short stories is published, he accepts a teaching position at … Iowa State, in their creative writing department. He and his partner, a doctor named Tim Miller, move there — live there — are happy there. Every so often, he goes to New York to meet with his publisher and calls his old boyfriend, Ethan Keene. They get together for coffee. There's awkwardness, but they're —

ETHAN. *(To audience.)* — trying to be friends, but it's hard work, pretending you never loved someone. *(To Michael:)* Because I did, you know. *(Beat, then back to the audience:)* Ethan Keene keeps writing movies. His remake of *Eyes Without a Face* is filmed and released theatrically. When it gets terrible reviews, Ethan is only *mildly* devastated, because he's kept writing plays — some which get produced, some which don't. Which Ethan *refuses* to dwell on, because he's kept revising *himself*, struggling to make *himself* a deeper person, someone who's not afraid to slow down, take stock of his life, open himself up, and be — hurt. *(Beat.)* He makes mistakes, backtracks, learns the same lessons over and over again, but he leads a full and fulfilling life with … *surprisingly* little regret.

TYLER. Bro …

MICHAEL. I think it's about to start, Ethan …

ETHAN. *(To them.)* Okay, okay … *(To audience.)* This is a beginning, not an ending. Sometimes you have to tell yourself what to feel. *(He shows what he means.)* "I'm okay with this." "I'm starting to get better." "I'm happy today." *(Realizes.)* This has been — *(Thinks about it.)* — this has been a totally insane, totally terrible, totally wonderful couple of years.

MARY ELLEN. Ethan …

ETHAN'S DAD. Son …

ETHAN. *(To them.)* Okay, okay … *(Ethan moves to the back of the stage and takes his seat next to the others. The lights start to fade. As that's happening, a projector from behind the stage starts projecting a movie over our cast's — and the audience's — heads. Horror movie music starts to play. Ethan and the others watch, rapt.)* Totally to be continued — *(Quick blackout.)*

End of Play

PROPERTY LIST

Sheaf of papers
Laptop computers
Coffee cup
Shoulder bag
Cell phones
Nametag
Answering machine
Champagne, 2 glasses
Notes
Sunglasses, towel
Suitcase
Comic book
Book

SOUND EFFECTS

"Bling" noise
Cell phone rings
Phone hang-up
Subway sounds
Regular phone rings
Answering machine beep
Voice through answering machine
Answering machine recording
Horror movie music

NEW PLAYS

★ **GUARDIANS by Peter Morris.** In this unflinching look at war, a disgraced American soldier discloses the truth about Abu Ghraib prison, and a clever English journalist reveals how he faked a similar story for the London tabloids. "Compelling, sympathetic and powerful." –*NY Times.* "Sends you into a state of moral turbulence." –*Sunday Times (UK).* "Nothing short of remarkable." –*Village Voice.* [1M, 1W] ISBN: 978-0-8222-2177-7

★ **BLUE DOOR by Tanya Barfield.** Three generations of men (all played by one actor), from slavery through Black Power, challenge Lewis, a tenured professor of mathematics, to embark on a journey combining past and present. "A teasing flare for words." –*Village Voice.* "Unfailingly thought-provoking." –*LA Times.* "The play moves with the speed and logic of a dream." –*Seattle Weekly.* [2M] ISBN: 978-0-8222-2209-5

★ **THE INTELLIGENT DESIGN OF JENNY CHOW by Rolin Jones.** This irreverent "techno-comedy" chronicles one brilliant woman's quest to determine her heritage and face her fears with the help of her astounding creation called Jenny Chow. "Boldly imagined." –*NY Times.* "Fantastical and funny." –*Variety.* "Harvests many laughs and finally a few tears." –*LA Times.* [3M, 3W] ISBN: 978-0-8222-2071-8

★ **SOUVENIR by Stephen Temperley.** Florence Foster Jenkins, a wealthy society eccentric, suffers under the delusion that she is a great coloratura soprano—when in fact the opposite is true. "Hilarious and deeply touching. Incredibly moving and breathtaking." –*NY Daily News.* "A sweet love letter of a play." –*NY Times.* "Wildly funny. Completely charming." –*Star-Ledger.* [1M, 1W] ISBN: 978-0-8222-2157-9

★ **ICE GLEN by Joan Ackermann.** In this touching period comedy, a beautiful poetess dwells in idyllic obscurity on a Berkshire estate with a band of unlikely cohorts. "A beautifully written story of nature and change." –*Talkin' Broadway.* "A lovely play which will leave you with a lot to think about." –*CurtainUp.* "Funny, moving and witty." –*Metroland (Boston).* [4M, 3W] ISBN: 978-0-8222-2175-3

★ **THE LAST DAYS OF JUDAS ISCARIOT by Stephen Adly Guirgis.** Set in a time-bending, darkly comic world between heaven and hell, this play reexamines the plight and fate of the New Testament's most infamous sinner. "An unforced eloquence that finds the poetry in lowdown street talk." –*NY Times.* "A real jaw-dropper." –*Variety.* "An extraordinary play." –*Guardian (UK).* [10M, 5W] ISBN: 978-0-8222-2082-4

DRAMATISTS PLAY SERVICE, INC.
440 Park Avenue South, New York, NY 10016 212-683-8960 Fax 212-213-1539
postmaster@dramatists.com www.dramatists.com

NEW PLAYS

★ **THE GREAT AMERICAN TRAILER PARK MUSICAL music and lyrics by David Nehls, book by Betsy Kelso.** Pippi, a stripper on the run, has just moved into Armadillo Acres, wreaking havoc among the tenants of Florida's most exclusive trailer park. "Adultery, strippers, murderous ex-boyfriends, Costco and the Ice Capades. Undeniable fun." –*NY Post.* "Joyful and unashamedly vulgar." –*The New Yorker.* "Sparkles with treasure." –*New York Sun.* [2M, 5W] ISBN: 978-0-8222-2137-1

★ **MATCH by Stephen Belber.** When a young Seattle couple meet a prominent New York choreographer, they are led on a fraught journey that will change their lives forever. "Uproariously funny, deeply moving, enthralling theatre." –*NY Daily News.* "Prolific laughs and ear-to-ear smiles." –*NY Magazine.* [2M, 1W] ISBN: 978-0-8222-2020-6

★ **MR. MARMALADE by Noah Haidle.** Four-year-old Lucy's imaginary friend, Mr. Marmalade, doesn't have much time for her—not to mention he has a cocaine addiction and a penchant for pornography. "Alternately hilarious and heartbreaking." –*The New Yorker.* "A mature and accomplished play." –*LA Times.* "Scathingly observant comedy." –*Miami Herald.* [4M, 2W] ISBN: 978-0-8222-2142-5

★ **MOONLIGHT AND MAGNOLIAS by Ron Hutchinson.** Three men cloister themselves as they work tirelessly to reshape a screenplay that's just not working—*Gone with the Wind.* "Consumers of vintage Hollywood insider stories will eat up Hutchinson's diverting conjecture." –*Variety.* "A lot of fun." –*NY Post.* "A Hollywood dream-factory farce." –*Chicago Sun-Times.* [3M, 1W] ISBN: 978-0-8222-2084-8

★ **THE LEARNED LADIES OF PARK AVENUE by David Grimm, translated and freely adapted from Molière's Les Femmes Savantes.** Dicky wants to marry Betty, but her mother's plan is for Betty to wed a most pompous man. "A brave, brainy and barmy revision." –*Hartford Courant.* "A rare but welcome bird in contemporary theatre." –*New Haven Register.* "Roll over Cole Porter." –*Boston Globe.* [5M, 5W] ISBN: 978-0-8222-2135-7

★ **REGRETS ONLY by Paul Rudnick.** A sparkling comedy of Manhattan manners that explores the latest topics in marriage, friendships and squandered riches. "One of the funniest quip-meisters on the planet." –*NY Times.* "Precious moments of hilarity. Devastatingly accurate political and social satire." –*BackStage.* "Great fun." –*CurtainUp.* [3M, 3W] ISBN: 978-0-8222-2223-1

DRAMATISTS PLAY SERVICE, INC.
440 Park Avenue South, New York, NY 10016 212-683-8960 Fax 212-213-1539
postmaster@dramatists.com www.dramatists.com

NEW PLAYS

★ **AFTER ASHLEY by Gina Gionfriddo.** A teenager is unwillingly thrust into the national spotlight when a family tragedy becomes talk-show fodder. "A work that virtually any audience would find accessible." *—NY Times.* "Deft characterization and caustic humor." *—NY Sun.* "A smart satirical drama." *—Variety.* [4M, 2W] ISBN: 978-0-8222-2099-2

★ **THE RUBY SUNRISE by Rinne Groff.** Twenty-five years after Ruby struggles to realize her dream of inventing the first television, her daughter faces similar battles of faith as she works to get Ruby's story told on network TV. "Measured and intelligent, optimistic yet clear-eyed." *—NY Magazine.* "Maintains an exciting sense of ingenuity." *—Village Voice.* "Sinuous theatrical flair." *—Broadway.com.* [3M, 4W] ISBN: 978-0-8222-2140-1

★ **MY NAME IS RACHEL CORRIE taken from the writings of Rachel Corrie, edited by Alan Rickman and Katharine Viner.** This solo piece tells the story of Rachel Corrie who was killed in Gaza by an Israeli bulldozer set to demolish a Palestinian home. "Heartbreaking urgency. An invigoratingly detailed portrait of a passionate idealist." *—NY Times.* "Deeply authentically human." *—USA Today.* "A stunning dramatization." *—CurtainUp.* [1W] ISBN: 978-0-8222-2222-4

★ **ALMOST, MAINE by John Cariani.** This charming midwinter night's dream of a play turns romantic clichés on their ear as it chronicles the painfully hilarious amorous adventures (and misadventures) of residents of a remote northern town that doesn't quite exist. "A whimsical approach to the joys and perils of romance." *—NY Times.* "Sweet, poignant and witty." *—NY Daily News.* "Aims for the heart by way of the funny bone." *—Star-Ledger.* [2M, 2W] ISBN: 978-0-8222-2156-2

★ **Mitch Albom's TUESDAYS WITH MORRIE by Jeffrey Hatcher and Mitch Albom, based on the book by Mitch Albom.** The true story of Brandeis University professor Morrie Schwartz and his relationship with his student Mitch Albom. "A touching, life-affirming, deeply emotional drama." *—NY Daily News.* "You'll laugh. You'll cry." *—Variety.* "Moving and powerful." *—NY Post.* [2M] ISBN: 978-0-8222-2188-3

★ **DOG SEES GOD: CONFESSIONS OF A TEENAGE BLOCKHEAD by Bert V. Royal.** An abused pianist and a pyromaniac ex-girlfriend contribute to the teen-angst of America's most hapless kid. "A welcome antidote to the notion that the *Peanuts* gang provides merely American cuteness." *—NY Times.* "Hysterically funny." *—NY Post.* "The *Peanuts* kids have finally come out of their shells." *—Time Out.* [4M, 4W] ISBN: 978-0-8222-2152-4

DRAMATISTS PLAY SERVICE, INC.
440 Park Avenue South, New York, NY 10016 212-683-8960 Fax 212-213-1539
postmaster@dramatists.com www.dramatists.com

NEW PLAYS

★ **RABBIT HOLE by David Lindsay-Abaire.** Winner of the 2007 Pulitzer Prize. Becca and Howie Corbett have everything a couple could want until a life-shattering accident turns their world upside down. "An intensely emotional examination of grief, laced with wit." *—Variety.* "A transcendent and deeply affecting new play." *—Entertainment Weekly.* "Painstakingly beautiful." *—BackStage.* [2M, 3W] ISBN: 978-0-8222-2154-8

★ **DOUBT, A Parable by John Patrick Shanley.** Winner of the 2005 Pulitzer Prize and Tony Award. Sister Aloysius, a Bronx school principal, takes matters into her own hands when she suspects the young Father Flynn of improper relations with one of the male students. "All the elements come invigoratingly together like clockwork." *—Variety.* "Passionate, exquisite, important, engrossing." *—NY Newsday.* [1M, 3W] ISBN: 978-0-8222-2219-4

★ **THE PILLOWMAN by Martin McDonagh.** In an unnamed totalitarian state, an author of horrific children's stories discovers that someone has been making his stories come true. "A blindingly bright black comedy." *—NY Times.* "McDonagh's least forgiving, bravest play." *—Variety.* "Thoroughly startling and genuinely intimidating." *—Chicago Tribune.* [4M, 5 bit parts (2M, 1W, 1 boy, 1 girl)] ISBN: 978-0-8222-2100-5

★ **GREY GARDENS book by Doug Wright, music by Scott Frankel, lyrics by Michael Korie.** The hilarious and heartbreaking story of Big Edie and Little Edie Bouvier Beale, the eccentric aunt and cousin of Jacqueline Kennedy Onassis, once bright names on the social register who became East Hampton's most notorious recluses. "An experience no passionate theatergoer should miss." *—NY Times.* "A unique and unmissable musical." *—Rolling Stone.* [4M, 3W, 2 girls] ISBN: 978-0-8222-2181-4

★ **THE LITTLE DOG LAUGHED by Douglas Carter Beane.** Mitchell Green could make it big as the hot new leading man in Hollywood if Diane, his agent, could just keep him in the closet. "Devastatingly funny." *—NY Times.* "An out-and-out delight." *—NY Daily News.* "Full of wit and wisdom." *—NY Post.* [2M, 2W] ISBN: 978-0-8222-2226-2

★ **SHINING CITY by Conor McPherson.** A guilt-ridden man reaches out to a therapist after seeing the ghost of his recently deceased wife. "Haunting, inspired and glorious." *—NY Times.* "Simply breathtaking and astonishing." *—Time Out.* "A thoughtful, artful, absorbing new drama." *—Star-Ledger.* [3M, 1W] ISBN: 978-0-8222-2187-6

DRAMATISTS PLAY SERVICE, INC.
440 Park Avenue South, New York, NY 10016   212-683-8960   Fax 212-213-1539
postmaster@dramatists.com   www.dramatists.com